PRAISE FOR
SEX: OUR BODIES, OUR JUNK

"If you absolutely must buy ONE sex book this year that is as informative as it is disgusting, THIS should be the one. Or not."

—Buck Henry, screenwriter of *The Graduate* and *To Die For*

"If I had only read this book when I first started having sex, its wit and wisdom would have changed my life in so many positive ways that I would have become the six-foot-tall blonde I was meant to be much, much sooner."

—Merrill Markoe, author of *Merrill Markoe's Guide to Love*

"Whether you're a sexual Einstein (know a lot, never have it) or a sexual Tiger Woods (great golfer, have lots of it), this book will hold tons of embarrassing revelations for you. Quickly buy it and take it home, because right now the bookstore security camera is watching you reading it."

—Bob Odenkirk, co-creator and co-star of *Mr. Show*

"Why, this book is incredible. I...I've never seen anything like it. Jane! Michael! Father! Aunt Sarah! Constable! Little Bill! Arsenio! Cookie! Come quick!!!"

—Robert Smigel, creator of "Saturday TV Funhouse," and Triumph the Insult Comic Dog

"So, so funny. This book disproves the old conventional wisdom that sex is a poor subject for humor."

—DC Pierson, author of *The Boy Who Couldn't Sleep and Never Had To*

"A hilarious guide to all things physical. Until the day our souls shed the disgusting meat caskets known as 'the human form,' *Sex: Our Bodies, Our Junk* will serve as the North Star for all things wiener-related."

—Tom Scharpling, radio host, *The Best Show on WFMU*

SEX:
OUR BODIES,
OUR JUNK

THE ASSOCIATION FOR
THE BETTERMENT OF SEX
PRESENTS

SEX:
OUR BODIES,
OUR JUNK

Scott Jacobson, Todd Levin,

Jason Roeder, Mike Sacks,

and Ted Travelstead

BROADWAY BOOKS
NEW YORK

All rights reserved.
Published in the United States by Broadway Books, an imprint
of the Crown Publishing Group, a division of Random House, Inc., New York.
www.crownpublishing.com

BROADWAY BOOKS and the Broadway Books colophon are trademarks
of Random House, Inc.

Library of Congress Cataloging-in-Publication Data
Sex: our bodies, our junk / by the association for the betterment of sex,
Scott Jacobson . . . [et al.].
p. cm.
1. Sex—Humor. I. Jacobson, Scott. II. Title.
PN6231.S54S394 2010
818'.602—dc22 2010003636

ISBN 978-0-307-59216-3

Printed in the United States of America

Design by Maria Elias

10 9 8 7 6 5 4 3 2 1

First Edition

The authors would like to thank Michelle Brower and Christine Pride for seeing this book through from the beginning; Michael Faisca, Nick Gallo, and Bob Sikoryak for their beautifully indecent visuals; Michael Kupperman, Andy Richter, Allison Silverman, Sarah Thyre, and Jon Wurster for upstaging us every other chapter; Laura Griffin for hours spent trolling for photos; S. P. Nix for his top-notch editing skills; and Georgia Haege for putting up with being our muse.

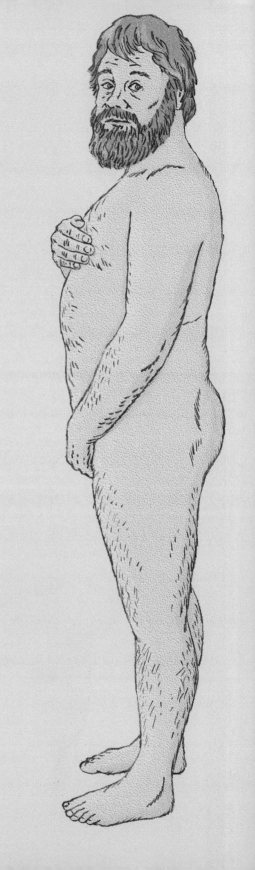

CONTENTS

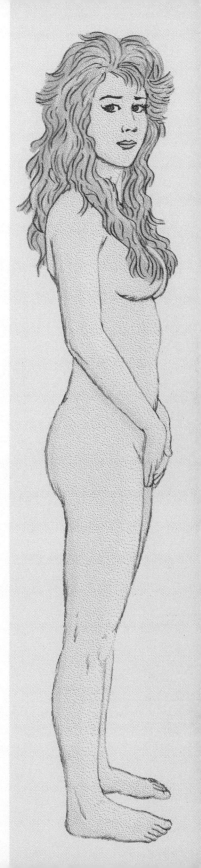

FOREWORD

Andy Richter and Sarah Thyre are a married couple. They have participated in several ABS-sponsored Marriage Fresheners/Bow-and-Trap-Hunting Survival Weekends.

FOREWORD FOR THE FELLOWS!

By Andy Richter

As I write this, my wife, Sarah, and I are a week away from celebrating our sixteenth wedding anniversary. Few of our peers enjoy a relationship that boasts the same longevity, and we are frequently asked for the secret to our success. Well, there isn't really a secret, but the authors of this book still valued our experience enough to ask us to write the foreword you're reading now.

Of course, one of the most important facets of any lasting relationship is an ongoing, evolving, mutually enriching sexual life. Over the years, I have learned a thing or two about what it takes to keep things sexy between me and my beautiful wife. However, as I can only truly speak from the male perspective, I'd like to confine my advice to the men out there. So, fellas, here are a happy hubby's tips for a healthy sex life—a sex life in which she gets what she wants, and you get what you *need!*

1. **LOCATION:** First, you've got to pick out the places in which you will be masturbating. As a husband, these "jerk zones" will become your oases in the desert of your life. The criteria for these areas should be self-evident: adequate privacy, plausibility in regard to elapsed time of session, and access to tissues. An out-of-the-way powder room is a perfect example. The shower can be great depending on traffic patterns (i.e., those fucking kids barging in every time you try to get one minute of peace), and it negates the tissue issue. And don't

rule out the workplace. If you're lucky enough to have your own office with a locking door, you're golden. No one ever questions a supposed "conference call." I would recommend, however, that you place any family photos outside of your midstroke field of vision.

2. **TIMING:** Once you know where you're going to beat off, you've got to know when. Being reactive is the key. Get to know your wife's patterns, and look for those times when she will be reliably occupied. School drop-off, leg-shaving, a phone call to or from her sister: all of these can be your moment to get that well-deserved nut. And, by all means, remain flexible! Your mate's last-minute run to the grocery store can be your green light to a delightful impromptu knob-polishing.

3. **KEEP IT SIMPLE:** The more self-sufficient you are in your pud pulls, the better off you'll be. Try to keep your masturbatory accessorizing to a minimum. Sure, everybody loves porn, but toting a laptop to the bathroom so you can "check your email on the crapper" will eventually arouse suspicion. Use your imagination! Replay some old episode from your past, or try to picture what's going on beneath the long underwear of the models in the Lands' End catalog. Or get an iPhone. Lubricants other than saliva are okay so long as they are a native part of your jerk-zone environment, but be careful of untested lotions and conditioners. Steer clear of anything labeled "renewing" or "glycolic"; that shit burns your pee-hole like a motherfucker. And for Christ's sake, don't get fancy! Never forget that the threat of discovery is always present, and it's much easier to explain away a plain old vanilla meat-beating than it is to make her okay with catching you with a hair brush up your ass.

This is just a start. As you progress in your married sex life, you will make discoveries of your own; you'll find out what's right for your situation. I hope I've helped open your mind to the possibilities that exist when you're willing to work at it. Remember, in a marriage, keeping your sex life satisfying is truly up to *you*.

FOR THE LADIES (AND THE FEMALE-IDENTIFYING HETEROSEXUAL TRANSGENDERIES)

By Sarah Thyre

I'm sure my husband, Andy, has given the boys some sensual yet sensitive tips for keeping the marital juices flowing. But it's important to remember that "relationship" can't be spelled without two "I"s. Ladies, I would like to give you some helpful hints to pass on to your partners. Because, as we all know (conspiratorial wink), they need all the help we can give!

There are four simple reminders that men need to see, preferably printed in an unadorned, sans serif font (I recommend Helvetica—the name itself might remind your man of the childhood nanny he never had). Post several copies in key locales throughout the home: on the bathroom mirror, the refrigerator, the lotion drawer. Herewith, in order of importance:

1. **PUT YOUR PLATE IN THE *DISHWASHER*,** not the sink. The dishwasher is conveniently located right next to (or very near) the sink, where you left your plate. The dishwasher has a handle.

2. **DON'T EXPECT A THANK-YOU FOR DOING THIS.** Instead, expect the phrase "Could you at least . . ." to precede most every request I make of you. Expecting this is really the least you could do.

3. **SOMETIMES YOU MAKE MY SKIN CRAWL.** Other times the smell of your sternum fills me with passionate intensity. These sensations might occur simultaneously.

The fourth and final tip should be posted in a minimum 20-point font size, all caps, bold italicized and double underlined. There's something men just don't say enough, and really, there's no excuse. The message is clear on every billboard, in every movie, TV show, ballad, and Lyndon LaRouche pamphlet, even in the olde tyme-y tune-a-roonies they still warble down at the Shim Sham Club. It's something every girl dreams of hearing from her very own Prince

Charming. I've been with my Prince for eighteen years, sixteen of those non-sinfully. During all that time, you'd think that my otherwise caring, kind, and considerate mate would have said the magic words more than once or twice, or three or four times, however many I'm not exactly sure. . . . *anyhoo*, we hate having to ask them to say it, don't we? It sounds so pathetic, and it makes us feel they are not in touch with our needs. I'm referring, of course, to the verbal expression of ultimate intimacy. To wit, the fourth reminder:

4. **AT LEAST ONCE A DAY, LOOK DEEPLY INTO MY EYES AND SAY THE FOLLOWING: "DARLING, I'M GONNA SHOOT MY GARBAGE IN YOU."**

By this time, you're probably thinking, "Whoa, Sarah, what are we doing here, reappropriating the concept of a 'nag' and using it for our own postfeminist, sex-positive, liberated-from-shame purposes?" Yes, ladies (and transgenderies), that's exactly what we're doing. But remember: Every relationship benefits from a little quid pro quo, so I've got one more tip for you:

Don't be afraid to use the word "cock." Say it out loud, let it roll out one side of your mouth like an errant dribble of Chardonnay. If it makes you uncomfortable, try imagining that you've lost your tongue in an industrial accident and are just saying "clock." That oughta do it.

There now. Onward to sexual success!

INTRODUCTION

By the Association for the Betterment of Sex

TOWARD A RADICAL NEW UNDERSTANDING OF SEX AND INTIMACY

We don't talk about sex in this country, not like we should. Think about it: You can conduct an entire transaction with a clerk at Enterprise Rent-A-Car and have no idea how orgasmic she is. And if we don't talk about it, how on earth are we supposed to *learn* about it? What most of us know about sex—what most of us *think* we know, anyway—was probably acquired through some confused mixture of middle-school curriculum, pornographic playing cards, and bits and pieces overheard from the conversations of homeless people. There are even stories of couples—adults, mind you—who avoid oral sex for fear that the woman will become pregnant, as if they've never heard of dental dams!

You probably know better, of course. But do you know all you *need* to? Let us answer that question: *not yet.*

We at the Washington, D.C.–based Association for the Betterment of Sex (ABS) have written this manual with a very specific reader in mind—*you!* Man or woman, gay or straight, young or old, but not grotesquely old, this is the one and only intimacy resource you will ever need. As you pore over the following pages, you will soon come to realize that your entire library of sexual guidebooks—from the classic *Joy of Sex* to the underappreciated *Sexual Potency Through Santeria* to the massively influential *Wieners and Woo-Woos*—aren't good for much more than propping up your kitchen table or elevating your lover's backside for ease of penetration (see p. 79, fig. 3). In short, you're holding a book like no other.

What makes it so special? Simple. The ABS approach. Maybe a story will help. There was once a group of blind men, each of whom touched an elephant on a different part of its body— the trunk, the tusk, the rear. Because each man had a different experience, each had a unique, yet valid, take on what an elephant actually was.

Now imagine the "elephant" is actually a fourteen-inch textured dildo called Big Tex. Or the do's and don'ts of fisting at high altitudes. Or whether it's still considered safe to store your condoms in Barbicide. Sexual truth is never a constant—it varies from one mature, engorged partner to the next. It's up to you to decide what turns you on and what gives you AIDS. We're here not to judge you but to *guide* you. To gently take your hand while you're having sex, and to then sit on a bedside stool, patiently waiting for you to finish. Let us be your blind men.

What makes us qualified for this task? Let's look at the stats. Between the five of us, we have:

8,753 hours of intercourse experience (hereafter referred to as logged insertion hours, or LIHs)

14,350 hours of foreplay

12,322 hours of snuggling

9,002 hours of therapeutic post-sex "hold 'n' cry"

752.5 hours of light spanking

3 hours of heavy spanking

378 fetishes (counting only those recognized by Western science)

1,000 minutes of feather play

578 pounds per square inch of combined back-massage pressure (CBMP)

1,246 collective hours of listening to Lenny Kravitz tunes

And, as of the time of this writing, 6,576 hours of "in" . . . not to mention 7,390 hours of "out"

But no matter how impressive these numbers are, they can reveal only so much. Allow us to introduce ourselves—the soft, fleshy faces behind the statistical data:

Head researcher **Dr. Michael Sacks** earned a B.A. from the University of Phoenix, a master's in psychology from Tulane University, in New Orleans, and a Ph.D. in communications from the University of Maryland, Baltimore campus. He is the author of sixteen academic papers on sexuality, four of which have been published, including "Doin' It Clean: When Is the Appropriate Time to Tell Your Ex-Wife You Have VD?" and "The Advantages and Disadvantages of Puberty: A Schematic Look at the Distinctions Between Child and Adult, in Relation to Vladimir Nabokov's *Lolita* and John Hughes's *Some Kind of Wonderful.*"

From 1991 to 2001, Sacks worked as vice president of communications at the Fullerton Institute, a think tank in Alexandria, Virginia, that provides MTV and other music-video companies with the latest up-to-date information on urban sexual practices and lingo.

In 2001, Sacks published an award-winning children's book called *Stuart*, about a gentle, carefree African American pimp who wears dress socks and likes to perform magic tricks.

Sacks enjoys horseback riding and listening to NPR's *Wait, Wait, Don't Tell Me* while exercising. He lives in Potomac, Maryland, with his wife, Sandra (shopping-advice columnist for the *Potomac Almanac*), and their three children, Zach, Brandon, and Gooch. He joined the Association for the Betterment of Sex as chairman of erotic touch in the spring of 2003.

Scott Jacobson trained as a urology clinician at the University of South Florida. In the 1990s, Jacobson challenged the presiding orthodoxy of the medical establishment with his admission that urologists—Jacobson emphatically included—get aroused by their work.

This wake-up call, issued on the highly popular, currently defunct public-access show *Talkin' Tubes with Dr. Scott*, transformed

Jacobson into a urology outlaw. His bold follow-up editorial ("Gyne-cologists Like It, Too," *Key West Keynoter*, April 6, 1997), as well as signed-postings on several Usenet groups devoted to genital har-nesses, attracted the attention of the Florida Board of Medicine.

Today, Jacobson is an accredited urological healing profes-sional practicing a personally devised, Eastern-influenced system of massage-based urinary therapy at his clinic in Takoma Park, Maryland. Through stroking, light pinching, "scold slaps," and other forms of noninvasive touch, Jacobson achieves serious results with a minimum of swelling and infection. He lives in Takoma Park with his partner, "straight chiropractor" Linda Frigolette, and their ad-opted teenage son, Trang.

Jacobson joined ABS in 2005 as a tenderness consultant.

At birth, **Todd Levin** was afflicted with pre-pubertal progeria, an extremely rare genetic condition that rapidly accelerates sexual development. By the age of four, Levin possessed the secondary sex characteristics of a twenty-five-year-old man. After spending a child-hood hounded by sensationalist media and scorned by conservative watchdog groups, Levin developed a crippling, mute-like introversion.

On his sixteenth birthday, Levin claimed emancipation from his parents and immigrated to Europe. There, his sexual precoc-ity was celebrated in the nightclubs and cabarets of Paris, where he soon learned to overcome his shyness through the timeless art of burlesque. Billed as "La Ventriloque Sexuelle," he performed a much talked-about *duo de comédie* that involved throwing his voice and manipulating the opening of his penis like a small mouth. Au-thor Gore Vidal raved that Levin's "relationship with 'Tati,' a flaccid penis sporting a tiny bowler hat (a coy nod to René Magritte's 'Son of Man'), is akin to the relationship between *la grande tristesse* of the human condition and the naïveté of hope. It doesn't hurt that Levin can work his meatus like a 2,000-baht-an-hour Thai hooker."

Satisfied with a fleeting taste of fame, Levin returned his atten-tion to his studies, eventually earning a Ph.D. in erogenous geogra-phy from the University of Delaware, online campus.

Today, Levin divides his time between caring for his pair of scarlet macaws and teaching a survey-level course on sexual hygiene at Montgomery Community College, in Rockville, Maryland. He is also the co-inventor of the Ripped 'n' Ready Virtual Squats Exertainment System, available exclusively at ESPN Zone Europe.

Levin joined ABS in 2004 as director of community outreach.

Jason Roeder was raised by Peace Corps volunteers who ran a one-room schoolhouse that frequently collapsed upon the children of a small village in Tanzania. As a result, Roeder was a citizen of the world at an early age, despite being the only one in his peer group who had white skin and hoped that Tom Petty would soon play the savanna.

As Roeder grew into adulthood, things began to change. His parents returned to the United States to realize their dream of opening a mailbox store, while most of his indigenous friends moved on to family life and whittling small tribal figurines designed for the desks of therapists. Suddenly Roeder had seemingly lost his sense of place in the world: Who was he? Where did he belong? He avoided these questions by masturbating furiously, every day, for many months, in the shade of his favorite acacia tree. It was then he realized his calling: "I'm surrounded by poor, malnourished people who have no idea what Kegel exercises can do for their orgasms. I will make this right."

Roeder promptly left for the United States to begin his self-designed program in cross-cultural sexology at the Florida Academy of Intimate Arts, now destroyed. His first book, *The Sex Tourist's Guide to the Everglades*, was published in 2004 by a small Jacksonville, Florida, press called Rise Up. At the time, he was unaware of Rise Up's emphasis on white-supremacist screeds.

Roeder joined ABS in 2006 as the group's chief of global initiatives and, when not on assignment abroad, lives in Poolesville, Maryland.

An only child of divorce, **Ted Travelstead** lived a latchkey existence through much of his childhood and adolescence. Many hours spent alone gave him plenty of time to explore every inch of his body with gentle, curious fingers and the detached, cold eye of a research scientist. As a teen he realized that when he was lucky enough to interact sexually with others, they were often amazed at his savant-like ability to locate their erogenous zones with a minimum amount of hints—and then stimulate them with incredible efficiency.

The following years found Travelstead on a sort of sexual walk-about, in a quest to possess as much carnal knowledge as possible. Falsely accused of arson at the age of thirty, he spent three years behind bars, but used this hard time to learn all he could about the sex lives of the incarcerated. He has collected these lessons in his book, *Serving 25 to Lust* (Bethesda Publishing), and hopes it will dispel many of the myths surrounding jailhouse intimacy.

Travelstead is also the founder of *Apples and Oranges*, a sex-education variety show geared toward middle-school students. It was while developing this show that he first donned a nude body stocking and morphed into his emcee character, Nude Billy. Now a sensation, Nude Billy will next be seen in The Touch Factory, a soon-to-be-released virtual reality game for special-needs adults.

Travelstead received an unpaid internship with ABS upon completing his parole, in 2001, and is now the head of the association's Field Studies Initiative. He lives with his wife and their two hounds, Kirk and Randy, on a ranch outside Elkton, Virginia.

So, after reading our author bios you now undoubtedly feel as if you know and trust us with the innocent vulnerability an infant shows his nursemaid. That's all we ask. Let your guard down and wipe away a lifetime's worth of accumulated inhibitions. In return we promise to teach you the way all those other stupid teachers couldn't have dreamed of teaching you. You will be taught as a sexy, intelligent person *deserves* to be taught. In fact, we'll make another promise: We are going to *keep* teaching you. And teaching you. And teaching you. Until you ask that we please stop. We might listen, we might not, but here's the thing . . .

We're going to *teach* you.

A NOTE ON SEX TERMINOLOGY, IN ACCORDANCE WITH 5,000 YEARS OF TRADITIONAL VALUES

If you happen to be reading this book in a part of the world where fundamentalist religious values hold sway and the discussion of sex is taboo, the following chart should help you to avoid angering your god or whomever it is you pray to when the lights are off and the TV is on the fritz.

WHERE YOU SEE . . .	REPLACE IT WITH . . .
Penis	Male area
Vagina	Lady's under-the-stomach place
Circumcision	The Lord's tailoring
Masturbation	Occasional spasmodic concession to Satan
Anal with reach-around	Anal with reach 'round

This list is by no means exhaustive. Any objectionable term not covered above should be substituted with the words "angel feathers."

CHAPTER 1

HUMAN SEXUAL ANATOMY

ARE YOU NORMAL? NO.

This chapter explores human reproductive anatomy in all its diversity, complexity, and occasional pronounced leftward curvature. As you read,

you might wonder how your own sexual organs compare with others of your gender. It's only natural. Whether we're scrutinizing the profiles of our erections in the bathroom mirror or the clefts of our vaginas in a bakery window, all of us at one time or another have asked ourselves if we "measure up." Well, there's no clear answer.

For one thing, variety is part of nature. Our bodies, while broadly guided by our evolutionary heritage, our individual genetic allotment, and our mother's prenatal drinking habits, are astonishingly differentiated. You may think you're the only one who spontaneously lactates every time it rains, but our research suggests that at least one other person on your bus does the exact same thing. Her name is Carol.

In addition, the very conception of "normal"—as well as the consequences of deviating from it—varies across cultures. In the North African nation of Mauritania, for example, women with a clitoral glans measuring less than a fifth of an inch wide can be fined heavily, while in western Mongolia, men with fewer than 150 scrotal dimples are generally outcasts who work local sideshows all their lives. On the other hand, in Sicily and Nova Scotia, an atomically small penis will barely be noticed as long as you do your share of the fishing. In other words, "fitting in" means something entirely different depending on where you're standing. If your genitals trouble you persistently, consider showing them to the staff of a foreign embassy or consulate. You might just discover that what you thought was strange or inadequate will hardly be noticed in a culture that's seven time zones away and a little more "out there."

But for all the variation found in human sexual anatomy, there are certain universals. That's where we'll begin.

THE PENIS:
AS GOOD AS IT GETS

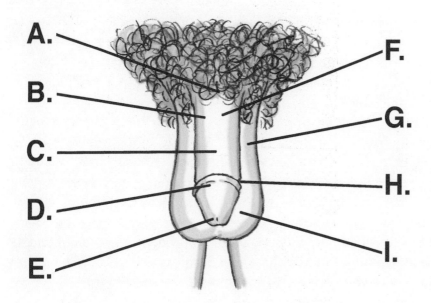

a) The O'Reilly factor
b) Roundtree's scepter
c) Sexaphone reed
d) Mr. Peanut's cane and hat
e) Poor man's off button
f) Randy dandy
g) Kickstand
h) Da demon's beak
i) Grippin' strip

THIS MOST CURIOUS OF MASCULINE BEASTS

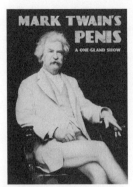

Mark Twain's Penis, the Broadway show for which Hal Holbrook did not win a Tony.

Strike up the band! From Toledo to Timbuktu, there's one body part everyone celebrates!

It greets each day with a sun salutation, announcing itself stiff and proud under boxer shorts, briefs, or wrinkled parachute pants. Sometimes terrible in its vein-bulging tumescence, other times meek and adorable as a panda cub, it is a curious beast. Indeed, there are few orifices or apertures it has not explored—human, animal, or lubricated mitten opening—yet how many can claim to know it in kind?

It is a talented appendage. What other body part can whirl joyfully like a helicopter? Or top *U.S. News & World Report*'s list of favorite body parts for almost twelve consecutive years?* Or star in its own hit Broadway show?

We speak, of course, of the penis. It has many other names, some of which demean it: weenie, dork, pee-pee, ding-a-ling. These should never be used. The only appropriate names communicate the strength and ruthlessness of a conquistador: pile driver, dog of war, pork sword, zipper shark, Patient X, Sammy Hagar.

As with any great natural gift, the penis comes with obligations. The average man spends at least an hour and a half each morning on penis grooming and upkeep, with frequent touch-ups throughout the day.

A typical hygiene regimen is as follows:

6:00 A.M.

Morning ablutions. From the initial sponge bath to a brief soak in Epsom salts and pat-down with a nice, fluffy towel, this phase is all about waking up the penis in a gentle, nurturing way.

---

*In a suspected case of gaming the system, the *frenulum labii inferioris* nudged the penis from the top spot in 1998.

6:30.

Shower time. The scalding hot water and harsh lathers found in a typical shower can unsettle the male genitals and are best kept away. To this end, a small, cylindrical shower cap is pulled over the penis.

A penis, sheathed and safe

7:00.

Powders, lotions, pastes, unguents, exfoliants—at this point, the penis hygiene regimen can get a tad complicated. Every man has his own preferred routines and products. Jim might swear by Dead Sea mud and eucalyptus vapors, while his friend Don prefers a bracing dip in a cold washbasin followed by a "tea sandwich" (gently pressing the penis between two organic cucumber slices). Experiment and figure out what works best for *you*. There is no wrong way to pamper the penis.

7:45.

Time to apply ornaments and accessories. This final phase is optional, as it is strictly a matter of taste. Many men enjoy tying ribbons around their penis or caparisoning it in hand-tooled leather straps and harnesses. Goth men sometimes outfit their penises with gargoyles and so-called penis armor. It's vital to remember that a man's penis ornaments do not necessarily reflect his sexual orientation. A man who paints elaborate henna-floral designs on his member is not necessarily gay, just as a man who streaks football eye black on his shaft and testicles is not necessarily straight.

Physiologically speaking, the penis is simplicity incarnate. Its parts resound like a poem. Do yourself a favor and read the following aloud:

Corona
Corpus Spongiosum
Glans
Prepuce
Ureeettthraaaaaa

Is there more to say about the workings of the penis? The process of erection? The elegance of design that allows for expulsion of urine and semen, but never both at once (unless it suits the penis's agenda)? Perhaps. But to say any more at this point would be an affront to the mystery of this most astounding and cherished sex organ.

AVERAGE PENIS SIZE:
TIME FOR A STATISTICAL RECENTERING

Let's be honest: Many of our male readers will open this book and flip straight to the section on average penis size. In fact, some probably have not purchased the book at all but are standing in the Sex and Relationships aisle at Barnes & Noble, methodically flipping to the "Average Penis Size" section in the hope that ABS will set the bar affirmingly, astonishingly low. If that's your game, then this is

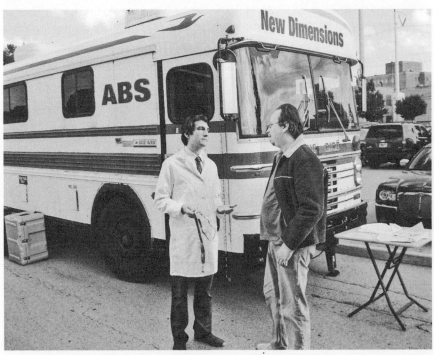

Shelby, Indiana: ABS researcher approaches a reluctant volunteer about participating in the measurement study.

not the book you're looking for—and, more important, other Barnes & Noble customers have figured out what you're doing and are growing increasingly uneasy.

Indeed, in the brief time sexology has existed as a scientific discipline, data on penis size have been all over the map. In 1948, Dr. Alfred C. Kinsey calculated the average penis length at 6.5 inches erect, with a girth of 5.5 inches. Masters and Johnson placed the number closer to 8 cubic feet, while Simon and Garfunkel arrived at a more conservative estimate: just 15 inches in length and 13.5 inches in circumference (see "The Boxer" for Garfunkel's specific research techniques).

These figures are all equally suspect and should not be taken seriously. Just as SAT scores were recalibrated in 1995 to reflect the growing stupidity of adolescents, it's time today for a wholesale statistical reevaluation of penis size. Last spring, ABS clinicians set off on a landmark coast-to-coast research expedition, measuring the flaccid, erect, and semisoft penises of 17,650 men of varying age, ethnic backgrounds, sexual orientation, and political affiliation. Perhaps we even passed through your town in "New Dimensions," our $1.2 million research vehicle recently acquired from the Lithuanian army.

We believe the results we gathered, while surprising, hold a mirror up to the nation's penises as they exist today.

We can be sure these numbers are accurate, not least of all because four of five ABS researchers, when measured, possessed these exact genitals. (The fifth ABS researcher has a reported "choad.")

WARNING:
If reading this book on public transportation, you should consider skipping the following pages.

THE AVERAGE PENIS

ERECT STATE
Length: 8.5"
Girth: 3.8" (shaft), 7.7" (head)
Above is an artist's rendering of the average American male penis, as determined by our survey. As you can clearly see, it has an exceptionally meaty fungiform head atop a slender shaft, the organ resembling in its entirety a modern sailboat anchor, or an L.L. Bean patio "sun-brella."

FLACCID
Length: 6.9"
Girth: 3.2" (shaft), 7.5" (head)
Here we see the average penis in its flaccid state. The proportions aren't too different. The shaft is slightly thinner and the head almost imperceptibly less meaty. Judging from this evidence, the celebrated distinction between "growers" and "showers" is not as pronounced as previously thought. Erect and flaccid penises are essentially the same.

If your penis looks nothing like the above illustrations, there's not much point in worrying about it. Statistics show that while 45 percent of men are unhappy with the size of their penis, only 7 percent of women express dissatisfaction with their partner's size. Of course, 0 percent of women know the truth about average penis size, as discovered by us. If you're a man reading this who's insecure about his genitals, try to hide this book from your lover or just switch the cover to something else, like a reference book on World War II aircraft.

MAKING YOUR PENIS APPEAR LARGER:
FIVE TRICKS YOUR PARTNER WILL PRETEND NOT TO SEE THROUGH

Still self-conscious about your penis size? You're not alone. Each year, 19,254 men worldwide undertake risky procedures designed to lengthen and thicken the penis—ligament slackening, silicone infusions, warthog-tusk grafts, and many others. The improvement is negligible, if any occurs at all, and the side effects can range from impotence to erections that point to magnetic northwest.

But while surgically increasing your penis length and girth remains elusive, there are a number of techniques you can employ to fool the eye and make your genitals appear more substantial. After all, you don't think men in pornographic films are really 10 inches, do you? Surprisingly, most are just 9.5 inches. The rest is an illusion achieved by simple household tricks available to practically anyone!

EUGENICS AND PENIS SIZE

Quite a few men have been led down the primrose path of breeding males in their family for optimal penis size. While selective breeding for desirable penis traits over multiple generations is indeed the only proven way to attain the heavy, swinging sex organ all men desire, the practice is not without drawbacks.

For instance, it's common knowledge that a child inherits his penis from his maternal grandfather. So it goes without saying that unless a man is familiar with everything science knows about the length, girth, shape (recumbent and erect), weight, vascularity, responsiveness to heat and cold, etc., of his lover's father's penis, he has no assurance that the penises of his own children will be up to snuff. It's Genetics 101, but try explaining that to your father-in-law when you show up on his doorstep with calipers and tailor's tape.

These are some of the most common:

1. **SHAVING YOUR PUBIC HAIR.** If your God-given penis length is lost in a skein of pubes, it's a good idea to shave as much off as you feel comfortable with. If your partner comments on your new look, just play it real casual and quip, "I happen to suffer genital alopecia due to a pituitary condition." If suspicion persists, quickly add, "Oh, hey! Gimme some groovy gravy," and then offer a high five. Your lover's gaze will surely be drawn away from the scabrous, razor-chapped deforestation crowning your sexual organ.

It's *always* the right time of year to sport
a penis sweater. (Actual size)

2. **LAYERING.** A bulky penile sweater can add up to 4 inches in circumference. But first ask your partner if she's aware of any cervical allergies to wool or rayon/cotton blends.

3. **FORCED PERSPECTIVE.** By making love before a mural of a foreshortened cityscape, your penis can appear to be the length of a side street or the height of a fifteen-story building.

4. **SMOKE AND MIRRORS.** Just like when magicians make the Eiffel Tower disappear, but in reverse.

5. **"HERBAL PENIS ENJANCE SPERM CANNON!!! BY MACHOMAX."** Received word about this in the ABS junk mail folder. Seems promising enough.

CIRCUMCISION: GOD'S PARTY FOUL

As a matter of standard hospital protocol, most American males nowadays are circumcised a day or two after they're born. Sure, there's always that one bizarre Jewish kid, or that creep in gym or Civics class, but you don't have to worry about their freak-ass kind.

In recent years, foreskin-rights groups have emerged to question the rush to snip (except in cases of hyper-prepucium, a condition in which the foreskin envelops the entire infant like a full-body sleeping bag and often leads to suffocation). These groups argue that the foreskin must have a purpose, because we were born with it. And even if it's one of those vestigial bits like the appendix, it's not often you see a man suddenly grimace and clutch his privates because his dong sheath just burst.

People on both sides of the debate have strong opinions (we're excluding a third group of fringe thinkers, who maintain that everything *but* the foreskin should be cut away). After all, while the foreskin naturally grows back on its own 23 percent of the time, thicker and nearly indestructible, circumcision is permanent for most males. So, what does the research tell us?

Our survey of 125 men attending last month's Annapolis Blue Angels air show suggests that there isn't a significant difference in terms of hygiene, susceptibility to disease, or sensitivity between the circumcised and uncircumcised, which would seem to argue against slitting a newborn's barely formed genitals with a scalpel or mohel's keychain. Whichever option you end up choosing, please resist the temptation to give your infant a "Prince Albert" genital piercing, even if the hospital *is* running a special that day.

THE VAGINA:

APOLOGIES TO THE SQUEAMISH

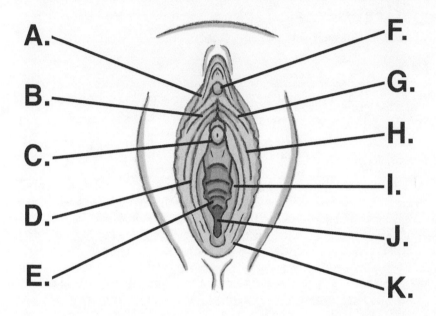

A.

B.

C.

D.

E.

F.

G.

H.

I.

J.

K.

a) Main puss

b) Auxiliary labia

c) Skid row

d) Cannery row

e) Val's hobby shop

f) Glitteris

g) Lé fountain of youth

h) Drifter's bus stop

i) Limeade stand

j) Mary Chestnut's bonnet

k) Devil's dustpan

ORIFICE OF SULTANS AND KINGS

While society teaches boys to be proud of their kingly genitals, it often sends the opposite message to girls, who grow up believing their pedestrian vagina is ugly or unclean. As with most sexual hang-ups, this one *can* be banished with proper education. From a young age, all girls should be taught that the vagina is not only special but a prize that has been avidly pursued by history's most powerful and courageous men.

From bloodthirsty warlord Genghis Khan and his estimated thousands of vagina conquests to Donald Trump and his sprawling, vagina-buttressed real-estate empire, generations of powerful males have enshrined the vagina as the ultimate symbol of manly potency. A 15-year-old girl filled with loathing toward her vagina during her period should remember that no less a personage than Julius Caesar liked vaginas very much indeed, and was proud to possess Cleopatra's exotic Egyptian vagina in 48 B.C. Similarly, a 27-year-old who is still too squeamish to let her boyfriend perform oral sex on her might instead imagine Christopher Columbus doing the job, or Benjamin Franklin, or feared sixteenth-century Aztec ruler Montezuma. As any reputable online encyclopedia will tell you, all were dedicated aficionados of the female genitalia.

Many young women are embarrassed by their bodies, and don't understand their historical importance.

George O'Keefe, like his sister Georgia, incorporated vaginal forms into his art.

Artists too have turned to the vagina for inspiration. Think Pablo Picasso, with his abstract, geometrical vaginas; Norman Rockwell's soda shop pudenda; or the vagina-crazed balladry of 1970s poet-songwriter Ted Nugent. Painter Georgia O'Keefe is famous for insinuating graceful vaginal forms into her paintings of dusty desert landscapes. Lesser known is her brother George O'Keefe, who took a more straightforward approach to the same subject matter.

For women who are aware of their vagina's place in history but still can't accept themselves as they are, there are a number of options. Dramatist Eve Ensler has written a series of monologues designed to be performed over six hours in a student-union basement and to beat a woman over the head with her own vagina until she at last breaks down and pledges loyalty to it. That production is a must-see, especially if you, like us, happened to catch the show the week it was performed by the incomparable Ruth Buzzi.

THE MYSTERIOUS CLITORIS:

THE VAGINA'S BIGFOOT

ABS receives thousands of letters on any given day. Once we've set aside questions that are too complicated or are directed to the paper towel company that happens to share our suite, the single question we receive most often has to do with that most elusive of human sexual parts, the clitoris (pronounced "kleet-a-rast," which is Latin for "mysterious" or "with incredible bewilderment"). Before we get to what we know about the clitoris, let us tell you what we *don't* know:

WHERE IT IS, EXACTLY

While we all know how to get to the clitoris—practice, practice, practice (LOL!)—we don't actually know where this female pleasure center is located or where it will show up next. *No one does*, even though the vast majority of experts might tell you differently.

Native Americans have, for many centuries, told fables of the clitoris. The Sioux speak of an eagle that descends from a giant explosion in the sky. He swoops down and, with his right talon, picks up an earthworm. He studies the worm carefully, a puzzled look on his face, and then drops it. He doesn't know what it is, and this frustrates him. He flies back up into the sky, wiser but no more knowledgeable about the clitoris than he was before.

In another legend, a Cherokee shaman calls a young squaw into his tent and asks her to disrobe. He very much wishes to see this extraordinary "knob of heaven" he has heard so much about from friends and

THE CLITORIS, AS VARIOUSLY DESCRIBED TO A POLICE SKETCH ARTIST

"Kind of a glistening inchworm."

"It was like a Caucasian gumdrop, mid-twenties."

"I don't remember too much, because it was pretty dark and I was drunk. I think it was wearing a hoodie, though."

"Sorry. Rule one of cunnilingus: don't snitch."

"I'd say it was about seven inches, with a bulbous, spongy tip that—hey, wait a second . . ."

"Big sucker: six foot three, maybe 210 pounds. Loads of Aryan tattoos."

from fellow shamans. "No," the squaw replies, "I cannot do so." "Why not?" asks the shaman. "Is it because of your shyness?" "I am not shy," says the girl, "but I *am* frightened of you." "Really? Is it because I am splashed from head to toe in the aroma of beaver urine?" "Yes," replies the girl, backing slowly out of the tent. The shaman sighs. No big deal. He'll just have to now ask Guy-Who-Lives-Down-by-the-Creek-Who-Claims-He-Once-Touched-It.*

Though much about the clitoris remains a dark mystery shrouded in what looks to be some sort of natural hood, there are a number of things we *do* know for certain:

- It's about the size of a bell pepper.
- Tastes a bit like fennel.
- When angry, spits out a red dye that stings.
- Is very, very timid but will brighten when it is sung to (especially doo-wop).
- Prefers "Blue Moon" to "Who Put the Bomp."

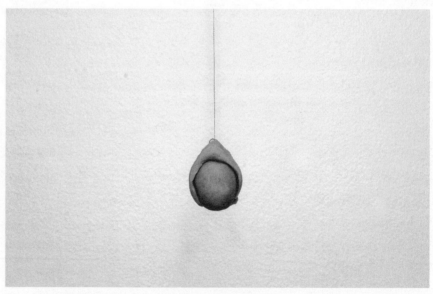

Only one photo has ever been shot of a clitoris, now confirmed to be faked.

*By the way, thank you, interns, for translating these two ancient Native American passages found framed on a TGI Friday's wall. Terrific work!

JUDGING THE CHARACTER OF YOUR GENITALS
ON THE HARRISON FORD SCALE

No two sets of genitals are completely alike, and the same could be said of the many roles played by the late, great Harrison Ford. It is interesting to note that the actor, ever the professional, always had his own genitals cosmetically modified according to the role he was playing. It is by using Ford's own methods that sexologists have determined that all genitals fall neatly into one of the following categories:

Zabriskie Point (uncredited)

Like Harrison Ford's uncredited "airport worker" in this 1970 Antonioni film, your genitals are unremarkable in every way—but no less hard-working for it.

Star Wars trilogy (Han Solo)

Reckless and rough around the edges, but undeniably charming, your genitals have an incredible magnetism but just can't keep themselves out of harm's way.

Regarding Henry (Henry Turner)

Your genitals recently absorbed the full impact of a .38 caliber bullet. And yet, somehow, amazingly, they've never operated better. In fact, they never fail to impress others—albeit in a tender, mentally challenged sort of way.

The Fugitive (Dr. Richard Kimble)

Others may fail to appreciate the better qualities of your genitals, but that's only because someone else has framed your genitals for a grisly murder. Do not give up hope, though—your genitals will be vindicated, even though your anus might remain suspect.

Patriot Games (Jack Ryan)

Dependable and solidly patriotic. After a while, however, one can't help noticing how your genitals appear to be stretched a bit thin.

Air Force One (President James Marshall)

At first glance, the differences between your genitals and the "Jack Ryan" are almost imperceptible. Take a closer look and it quickly becomes apparent that your genitals possess a far broader appeal. Your genitals could one day be president and, in fact, many already believe that they are.

BREASTS:
FUNBAGS OF MOTHERHOOD

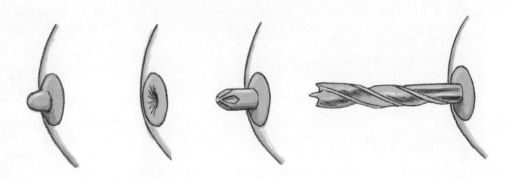

Common nipple types: protuberant, concave, Phillips head, 5/16″ brad point.

Are breasts sexual organs? That depends on whom you ask: a baby suckling milk from her mother would tell you no, while a man deliriously masturbating to a nipple faintly visible in the bra worn by a mannequin torso at Sears might tell you otherwise. But why should it be one or the other? If additional body parts can serve both pragmatic and erotic purposes (viz., the vagina's ability to break down certain starches and the penis's usefulness in scattering horseflies), why not breasts?

The breast is composed of three parts:

1. **THE NIPPLE.** The small, nerve-rich protuberance crowning the breast. It should be noted that while men's nipples are far less sensitive than those of females, they conduct electricity 37 percent better. Contrary to legend, there is no proven link between nipple type and social rank among humans.

2. **THE AREOLA.** The colored ring that spreads out from the base of the nipple; the saucer to the nipple's teacup, or the Packers coaster to its tallboy of Moosehead. Its diameter can range anywhere from an eighth of an inch to roughly that of a stop sign.

3. **BREAST "FILLER."** Generally classified as the best part on which to tattoo a dolphin.

While all breasts share these components, they demonstrate considerable variation in size and shape. No size or shape is more functional than another (with the exception of rare drape-like breasts, which allow limited gliding), but, nonetheless, women are often insecure about their bosoms. That's why a true gentleman reassures his date by telling her that whatever her breasts may look like or however her nipples are shaped, he will greet them each and every time with tears of gladness and the words, whispered to each nipple in turn, "Thank you for being exactly what you are. I am passionate about you!"

A READER ASKS...

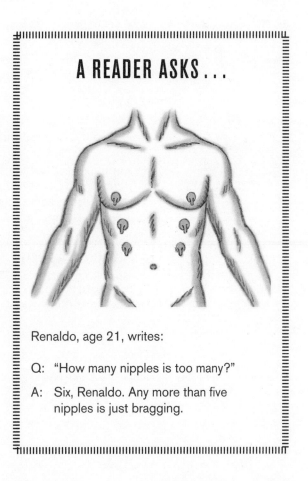

Renaldo, age 21, writes:

Q: "How many nipples is too many?"

A: Six, Renaldo. Any more than five nipples is just bragging.

GENITAL SELF-EXAMINATION CHECKLIST

It's hard to believe, but many men and women have never taken a good close look at their own genitals. If this describes you, the time for excuses ends now. Remove your dungarees and gather the following items:

The Geniflector
by Take-A-Peek

❑ **A HAND MIRROR**
Preferably a model made especially for genital examination, such as the popular Take-A-Peek brand Geniflector ($29.99 at most Spencer Gifts and dollar stores). If a mirror isn't available, you can use fancy silverware, preferably a sharp, thick steak knife. If you must use a spoon, bear in mind that your genitals are probably not nearly as convex as they initially appear.

❑ **JEWELER'S LOUPE**
For examining the genitals' finer details, such as clarity, color, and the presence of fissures.

❑ **PLUMB LINE**
(penis only)
For determining the member's center of gravity.

❑ **PINHOLE CAMERA**
Needed only if genitals are occluding the sun.

❑ **FISH-EYE LENS**
Not necessary, but amusing.

❑ **A REGISTERED NOTARY PUBLIC**
To verify all observations and submit a copy to local, state, and federal authorities.

UNCOMMON ANATOMY:
PARTS OF DARKNESS

Who hasn't sat around a campfire with a gaggle of cousins, uncles, half brothers, and stepsisters, listening to wild stories about sexual freaks that have been passed down from generation to generation, originating from the old country? ABS went out into the field and collected some of the more memorable.

The Olegg

This gentleman, known only as "the Olegg," lived at some point in the late seventeenth century and was, by all accounts, a simple farmer endowed with nine penises at various intervals around his waist. Legend has it that he could use these to prop himself up within the mouth of a well for just long enough to eat an entire melon.

The Olegg in his
natural habitat

Carla from New Hampshire

In the mid-1980s there were quite a few sightings of a woman from New England whose vagina could reportedly engulf and chew a medium-size sweet potato, all the while singing "Don't You Forget About Me" and performing basic accounting on an abacus.

The Vomiting Snake of Buford County

This disembodied penis would crawl the dusty back roads of Foster County, North Dakota, leaving a slimy trail. If confronted, it would become extremely rigid, and if poked or prodded, it would discharge venom a distance of fifteen yards. It was said to have once invaded a traveling tinker's bum in his sleep.

ANATOMICAL CHANGES IN A LIFETIME:

FROM THE INNOCENCE OF A CHILD TO THE CHAPPED HORROR OF OLD AGE

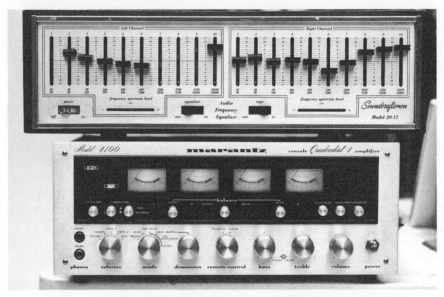

The female genitalia, seen at middle age

As we grow from infancy into adulthood and then into unspeakable old age, the human body naturally endures certain changes. Think of your body as a brand-new hi-fi stereo system. Your body is sleek and flawless as you first remove it from its Styrofoam packing (i.e., the protective lake of blood and mucus that surrounds you within the womb). You can't wait to use it, although there are a few buttons and inputs that might require a bit of instruction. And, similar to your new hi-fi, some of those instructions will be confusing or incomplete, or written in Cantonese.

As you advance through childhood, you'll begin to get the hang of things. You're still too young to be a real music aficionado, but you'll certainly enjoy the occasional use of your body's more popular features. Of course, it's only natural that along the way your genitals will acquire a few nicks, scratches, and the occasional impulsively placed 99.5 JACK FM promotional decal.

Upon reaching adolescence, your curiosity about music borders on insatiable. You must use your hi-fi day and night. At first you'll listen to the same records over and over again, but soon this will no longer prove satisfying, and you'll begin seeking out more experimental sounds—music you've imported from Germany and the Netherlands, often by artists who have been banned in the United States and Canada. You'll feel guilty about this at first, but you'll quickly get over those feelings and grow so consumed by your deep, nearly self-destructive appreciation for music that nothing else will matter—not schoolwork, summer jobs, intimate relationships, or the wounded-animal-like cries of your own mother as she bangs on your bedroom door, begging you to leave the hi-fi alone for a few hours in order to rejoin your family for Father's intervention.

It is during this period of adolescence, often continuing through your twenties and well into your thirties and even early forties, that your hi-fi will endure much of its wear and tear. You will hardly notice, however, because you will be so incredibly focused on your hi-fi's ability to play one long-playing record after another, sometimes four or five records a night. But make no mistake—even the most state-of-the-art hi-fi system is incapable of standing up to that kind of abuse without suffering long-term damage.

This will become all too apparent as you crest the steep hill of middle age, when you can't help but notice that your hi-fi has lost some of its luster, and its performance has been severely compromised. Its buttons have loosened, and its casing has become warped and puckered. You find yourself visiting home-electronics websites and coveting newer hi-fis, tricked out with all the latest features. Sure, you can have your own weathered hi-fi tuned up, and perhaps have some of its parts tightened or replaced, but what's the point? It's just going to break down again.

Eventually, you lose interest in music altogether—in fact, the sound of young people listening to music actually enrages you—and your hi-fi will fall into such a state of neglect that you're no longer certain it even functions anymore. Inevitably, it will end up collecting dust on the shelf of a Goodwill donation center or abandoned at a curbside, to be kicked at by the neighborhood idiot child. Yes, the human body is a marvelous thing.

OUR BODIES, OUR JUNK BEDITORIAL:
The First Time I Saw a Stranger's Genitals

Dr. Michael Sacks, Ph.D., Chairman of Erotic Touch

Believe it or not, I did not see my first penis or vagina until I was out of college, and only then at a great distance, through binoculars, while perched on a hill in suburban Maryland, overlooking the National Institute of Mental Health. I was performing a study for my graduate degree, although (and this is somewhat embarrassing) I now forget what the crux of the study dealt with or what I was doing on that hill in the middle of an excruciatingly hot summer's day, reclining in a lawn chair and sipping from a big ol' jug of hard lemonade.

Ted Travelstead, Head of Field-Studies Initiative

When I think about the first time I saw someone else's privates, my mind wanders back to the simple days of frolicking. The jumping into daisies, the shooing of butterflies, the sniffing of roots, and the gang. Oh, these were days of wondrous joy! The smell of hay was always in the air, and fresh peaches leapt from the trees in bushels galore. By Jim, we had a grand time in the barn! Shadow tag and "The Hillclimber" were the order of the day, and freshly oiled muscles glistened in the noonday sun. At lunch we would all clamor to go over to Alejandro's, for he had rickets and was encouraged to eat large bunches of grapes. We would stuff ourselves on grapes of all varieties, stopping every so often to make the "kissing wine." It was here that I first spied another's pink. Alejandro's grandfather, Colonel Budge, suffered from the sorest of muscles due to his time in the battles, and one day as I walked upstairs to retrieve a sponge, I spied Colonel Budge propped on a stool in front of the upstairs picture window. He was wearing no clothes, and next to him sat a shining metal scrub bucket. As I had never seen a fully nude veteran before, I stood transfixed and watched him spread the thick contents of the scrub bucket onto his chest and thighs. It did not look like an easy job, the ash-colored paste falling off in clumps, the Colonel swearing and slapping himself, but when he was finished he sat back in the sunbeams pouring through the window and let out a long, relieved sigh. In a matter of minutes he was snoring quietly, and it was then that I decided to risk a caning by taking a closer look. I tiptoed down the hallway to the room and stopped just past the door's threshold, my eyes searching the unfamiliar terrain of this grizzled old buck. When I spied the leathery serpent between his legs, I drew in a gasp that I thought would surely wake him. Never had I seen a front-tail of such length and girth! The gray old eel between his legs lolled halfway off the chair with its one eye slowly blinking, while I stared in wonder and fantasized about having a "pauper's whip" of such magnificence. Alas, this is where my memory gets hazy and I see only a static picture of a man hitting a tambourine.

Jason Roeder, Chief of Global Initiatives

Even though I grew up in a remote village in western Tanzania, I actually caught my first glimpse of nudity the way a lot of American boys did at the time. My friend Andongwisye told me he had something I just had to see, and he took me past the bathing pond, the nursing circle, and the circumcision plaza, until we finally came to a hollowed-out tree stump. When he took out an issue of National Geographic, I thought it was going to be the most boring thing in the world—but then I saw the pictures! Astonishing! The women were completely topless and weren't wearing much else otherwise! You would think I would have seen such nudity in person, but the women of my village were unusual in their fondness for microfleece pullovers.

Todd Levin, Director of Community Outreach

My first glimpse of another's genitals was an experience as singular and indelible as the first time I scored a slam jam in the sport of basketball, or the first time I felt the gentle tug of a stranger's arm inside of me.

Just shy of my sixth birthday—already a man, thanks to a rare hormone imbalance—I found myself watching a lovemaking scene from a pornographic film. Before my eyes, something new and brave was unfolding—a dense weave of fully engorged adult genitalia of every variety, pumping pneumatically. I was transfixed! So much so that it took several moments before I recognized a familiar stentorian voice, mere inches behind me: "You are in big trouble, young man!" I whipped around to meet my father's angry and accusing gaze. He boxed my ears and shouted, "You fool! You walked right into my shot! Now we'll have to relight!"

My father told the film crew to take a fifteen-minute cocaine break, and I was sent straight to my room. That night, I lay awake in my race-car-shaped bed, with the soft moans of pleasure reverberating against the walls of our paneled rumpus room and the faint perfume of saltpeter wafting up through the floorboards. In that moment, carnal ecstasy was sensually present yet infuriatingly elusive—similar to a yeti's bowel movement, or so I have read. Funny, but I wouldn't see a stranger's genitals again until much later that evening, when I entered the guest bathroom for a glass of water and accidentally interrupted a scene for another of my father's films, this one a serious documentary: Two in the Pink, and One in the Sink.

Scott Jacobson, Tenderness Consultant

I was privileged to grow up in a bohemian household, with a mother and father who adored the arts and prided themselves on putting their children in the glorious company of artists. At the age of nine, thanks to my parents, I found myself sharing a bunk bed for one magical autumn with Iggy Pop.

Before Iggy, I had never seen a man in "special pants." Which is to say I had never seen a man. It was a frosty morning in late September. My siblings and I trudged bleary-eyed to the breakfast table: "Hey, Mom, what's for breakfast?"

"How 'bout some pressed rat?" asked Iggy, falling out of the cupboard in his clear plastic trousers. The sight was startling: Uncle Ignatius's "rat," chubby and slumbering against the vinyl, was as bloated as if it had gorged itself on the very feast we children were pining for.

I remember wondering: Did that thing just eat our blueberry muffins?

HEY, DIDJA KNOW . . .

The amount of hair that covers the anus has no direct correlation to a man's or woman's IQ?

The nipple contains twenty-five bones, each of which can break and cause terrific, delicious pain?

The word *pussy* (when used to connote female genitalia) was first coined by Lewis, of Lewis and Clark fame?

The first marshmallows came from vaginas, and were a by-product of stress?

The smallest human penis on record came in at an astonishing 5 inches (Doug R., our summer intern, 2005)?

Men unconsciously follow baby-name trends when naming their penis? Hence the mid-00s prevalence of penises named Dashiell.

The most popular cake-related euphemisms for the vagina are (1) red velvet cake, (2) funnel cake, (3) pound cake, (4) Carvel Cookie Puss, and (5) double fudge birthday cake in the shape of Donkey, from *Shrek*?

The state of South Carolina still has laws on its books outlawing "flagrant and lewd displays of the epidermis"? And that many have been wrongly imprisoned, but the joke is simply too good to ruin?

CHAPTER 2

ATTRACTION

FULLY ENGORGED

MAGNETISM

If you asked a thousand men and women what they valued most in a sex partner, you'd get about as many different answers—a pretty face, broad shoulders, the girth of a Saturn V rocket, willingness to wear Mother's old girdle without a bunch of tiresome questions, and on and on. But advancements in the intimate sciences reveal that while we may think we have a thing for, say, redheads or the functionally illiterate, all of us, in fact, are hardwired to respond to certain cues passed down to us through hundreds of years of evolution. In fact, human sexuality provides some of the best evidence for the theory of evolution. Note the erotic thrill of draping oneself in animal skins and starting fires, or our love for Rob Becker's hilarious, informative play *Defending the Caveman*.

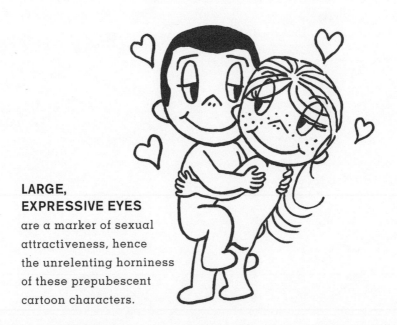

LARGE, EXPRESSIVE EYES are a marker of sexual attractiveness, hence the unrelenting horniness of these prepubescent cartoon characters.

If we want to fully understand what turns us on, we have to dig even deeper. There is no formula for physical attractiveness, though any large sampling of so-called conventionally attractive people will demonstrate some common traits, such as:

- Facial symmetry
- Large, expressive eyes
- Ear holes roughly the diameter of a Canadian dime
- A perineum no shorter than two middle-finger segments
- An areola circumference not exceeding that of the average bagel (female) or a jumbo, ooey-gooey cinnamon bun (male)

Of course, no discussion of attraction would be complete without the mention of nature's body spray, otherwise known as pheromones. While the data aren't conclusive, some scientists believe humans transmit a variety of sexual messages via odors released through sweat glands, and that to maximize the potency of pheromones it is best to never shower and to never be more than an hour removed from working on a chain gang.

The study of pheromones in humans is relatively new, but our research has tentatively identified three basic types:*

1. **AROUSAL.** A person's eagerness to engage in sexual congress.
2. **DESPERATION.** The extent to which a person yearns to not spend another Saturday night alone, listlessly masturbating during the commercial breaks of his or her favorite TV murder mysteries.
3. **CREEPINESS.** The likelihood that a person operates a citywide array of toilet cams.

*Epidermal secretions were clandestinely swabbed from twenty-five Olive Garden customers and then quickly analyzed in the men's room.

In addition, a variety of organic and synthetic pheromones have been marketed in the past few years, each intended to simulate natural pheromones that trigger arousal response in potential mates. These should be treated with great skepticism, however, as they are at best placebos and at worst dangerous. (One promising exception is a product manufactured by eurolotterybank@sexchannel.ru and sold under the claim that "this nice formula will make her want to bounce on the lovehammer until everyone moan!!!")

Now that you fully understand the science of attraction, let's talk about meeting people.

THE PICKUP LINE:
THE SEXUAL HOWDY

There is but one chance to make a first impression. This would especially hold true if you were, say, a doctor who arrives for surgery wearing a party sombrero with a stitched, anatomically correct donkey on its brim.

When you think about it, sexuality isn't much different. How many times have you been in the mood for a little "sumthin' sumthin'" and proceeded to chat up a potential lover, only to discover—perhaps within the first few moments—that the situation wasn't going as you'd hoped? Something was slightly off. Was it you? Your potential lover? The fact that you were both trapped beneath four hundred tons of rubble? Or was it something you actually said?

Language can be a tantalizing and effervescent tonic, but it can also be as repellent as a can of Miller Chill. What follows are examples of pickup lines to avoid, each carefully and scientifically tested before numerous focus groups consisting of males and females, 18 to 55 years of age, with one seventyish stranger named Louis only there for the free cubed cheese.

We recommend that you study and memorize each of these lines. In no particular order:

1. "You might recognize me from your window."
2. "You're not going to believe how many pig anuses the average hot dog contains."
3. "Quick: name your top five favorite Phil Collins tunes."
4. "Sit back, relax, and allow me to explain the importance of composting."
5. "I don't really see why we need art."
6. "I'm not one to brag, but I live on one of the largest houseboats on Lake Minnetonka."
7. "Listen, I know neither of us is racist, but humor me for a second . . ."
8. "Who do I have to fuck at this party to find out where to take a shit?"
9. "Is it hot in here, or is my body just completely covered in petroleum jelly?"
10. "Pretty real-looking for a prosthetic nose, huh?"
11. "Let's cut the crap, shall we? How much is this gonna cost me?"
12. "I wouldn't call them actual voices. More like hyenas scratching at the walls of my brain."
13. [Applying hand sanitizer] "Nothing personal."
14. "Everything Smurfy over here?"
15. "Guess which part of me is made of solid gold?"
16. "They can quarantine me all they want, but I ain't wearing no face mask."
17. "I can see you're not one of those fake and shallow people, super-concerned about appearance."
18. "Do you come to this hospital chapel often?"
19. "Ordinarily I'm not the type to just walk over and chitchat with a total stranger. Bye."
20. "Listen, my daughter needs a kidney *real* bad."

Okay, then. Now that you have a good idea of what *not* to say, it's time to seek out a place in which to not say it.

PLACES TO DISCUSS OR INITIATE SEX

Suze would do anything to meet a man who treats her with an ounce of kindness for once in her loveless life.

We've all been there. Not you, necessarily, but us, the members of the Association for the Betterment of Sex.

It's a weeknight, around ten o'clock. We're sitting in O'Toole's Sports Bar and Grill, just around the corner from our Washington, D.C., headquarters. No more zucchini poppers to be seen. The taps have run dry. The fifteen TVs are all blasting a strange sporting event involving an orange ball, an elevated metal ring, and a LeBron. Totally empty, except for the five of us, each in our own world, each of us thinking about tomorrow's research study on how many euphemisms there are for receiving oral sex while sitting in an outhouse (about 424).

There is one lone female bartender, and her name is Suze, but we call her "Curves." She looks exhausted, with large, dark circles under her eyes and a pasty complexion that often reminds us of a character in Billy Joel's "Scenes from an Indian Restaurant"—the waitress who serves up a bowl of yellow or jasmine rice, depending on your particular mood that night.

We all love Curves so very, very much. But, even with that said, we wouldn't ever dare dream of approaching her; she's totally off-limits. Why? Let's just say that there are a million more appropriate places to discuss sexual matters than at a scuzzy sports bar in the Dupont Circle area of our nation's capital.

What we're also saying is that when it comes to initiating sex, it all comes down to just *three* simple things: location, location, location.

What are the other two things, you ask?

Setting.

Also, locale.

How to put this in layman's terms for the reader with a borderline-deficient sex IQ? Here goes. A successful pickup line is, not surprisingly, very similar to a fake-vomit novelty gag. This fake vomit is wonderful in its place . . . like, say, beneath your lover's hammock. However, it's not so fantastic when your lover resides in an old-age home and has a reputation for "whoopsies."

There's a time and place for everything. Let's get into specific examples.

PICK-UP LINE	IDEAL LOCATION	LESS-THAN-IDEAL LOCATION
"I would love to kiss you."	Atop the Eiffel Tower	Inside a corrugated tin hut, as you interview the leader of Aryan Nations for *Hadassah* magazine
"I love children, which is why it's extra-ironic that I'm legally required to stay at least 100 feet from them at all times."	On the beach at sunset, walking hand-in-hand with your lover	At a Dave & Buster's, while ignoring your date and double-teaming on the Dance Dance Revolution game with an Asian pre-teen
"You know, in this light, you look just like Mickey Rooney!"	Anywhere in Hollywood, where Rooney is still widely-regarded as a sexual icon	As you drive a 1983 Pontiac 6000 through the front gate of an exclusive country club, from which you were banished six months prior

When broaching the subject of sex, men in particular are often accused of relying on the "little brain," at the head of the penis, for all of their decision making. In truth, they would be better served by using their "big brain"—the one located farther along the penis, just at the base of the shaft. Failing that, they could always fall back on their "regular brain," especially when courting potential lovers in that most sensitive of environments: the boardroom.

"BREEZJARS" AND "LOCKYKNOCKS": A GLOSSARY OF PICKUP SLANG

Recent years have seen the rise of so-called pickup culture: a near-scientific approach to seduction, as espoused online and in books by eyeliner-wearing scholars with names like SugarSmax and Doc Dazzle. Since newcomers tend to find the colorful jargon of pickup culture a tad confusing, ABS has rounded up a grab bag of the most commonly used terms that can easily be employed by any rank-and-file loser.

- **WINGMAN.** A seduction partner who assists his friend in conquering a target. Also called a "trimzing," after Himalayan Sherpa Tenzing Norgay (wingman on the legendary sexpeditions of Sir Edmund Hillary).

- **WINGCROW.** A dummy fashioned from a sackcloth and a silken "clubbing shirt," and sprayed liberally with TAG body spray. (Note: used when no wingman is available.)

- **TRUMPING.** Telling a target "I heard dat!" after she compliments you. (Alternative: screaming "Booya!" before she ever says a word.)

- **SCRIBBLE-DIBBLING.** Paying a target $100 to write seven random digits on a piece of paper, in order to give other targets the illusion that you are a skilled pickup artist.

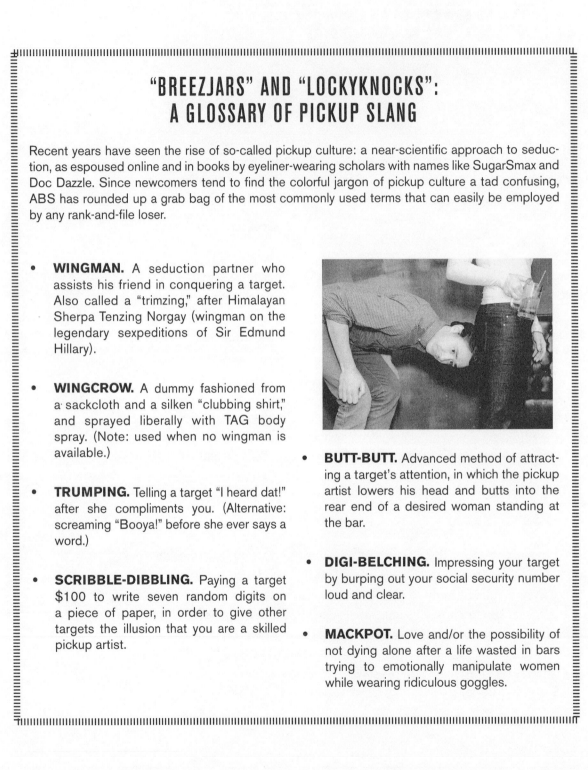

- **BUTT-BUTT.** Advanced method of attracting a target's attention, in which the pickup artist lowers his head and butts into the rear end of a desired woman standing at the bar.

- **DIGI-BELCHING.** Impressing your target by burping out your social security number loud and clear.

- **MACKPOT.** Love and/or the possibility of not dying alone after a life wasted in bars trying to emotionally manipulate women while wearing ridiculous goggles.

THE ABS GUIDE TO PEACOCKING

The peacock has to be one of God's strangest creatures: strutting around, so high and mighty, showing off a fistful of fancy feathers, acting like he's the dean emeritus of the University of Poontang. We here at ABS laugh ourselves silly just thinking about this idiotic monster. Relax, peacock! We humans may not have all that plumage, or the word *cock* in our name, but we do just okay for ourselves with our own extravagant symbols of beauty—and ours can be removed at day's end, not uncomfortably tucked beneath our rear ends in preparation for a sleepless night on a mound of petting-zoo straw.

My stars, just look at this fool.

It's not so difficult, this so-called peacocking thing . . . in fact, our patent-pending ABS method of attracting sexual partners through fancy dress and a convincing Drakkar smell-alike is *much* more effective than anything the good Lord above ever managed to screw up in all His infinite, non-university-degree "wisdom," or that Mother Nature managed to pinch out from between her rotten hindquarters.

That said, here is our foolproof method of attracting potential lovers, gleaned from solid, measurable research conducted in our mobile U-Haul behavioral-research facility (sadly, our "New Dimensions" vehicle broke down last week in a Hamburger Hamlet parking lot):

1. A Brunhilde helmet, with pigtailed wig, is a terrific way to meet exceptionally attractive women, especially when your face is covered in blue woad.
2. Carry an Irish boggle stick in your left hand. You'll never be at a loss for starting a conversation. Another solid opening gambit: "Look at my sack of homemade mustard!"
3. Wear discarded Kleenex tissue boxes on both feet. In a bind, desert sandals constructed from used Popsicle sticks work pretty well, too.

4. Corduroy breeches that have been ripped at both knees are a splendid conversation starter. Women are a curious lot. Often they'll tell you that they want their gentlemen to look "snazzy." On the other hand, they also like "bad boys." Split the difference and reach for perfection.

5. Sometimes your best friend on the dating scene is the heady, earthy scent you radiate. To achieve this effect, rotting deer meat hanging from each earlobe works marvelously (not pictured).

6. A T-shirt that reads GOD IS DEAD is ideal. ABS hesitates to even tiptoe into the realm of religion, but when the subject is as juicy as this one, it's practically irresistible. Alternative topic: "Did you see the fight outside? Wasn't that something? Also, where do you stand on the subject of the mentally retarded and forced abortion?"

7. Putting on one oven mitt is undeniably impish. This tells the world that you love to cook, but you're also kind of scattered. Women find this adorable, and they'll want to baby you—ideally, with hand sex.

8. It's an excellent idea to sport one single plumed feather (not pictured). Fall in love with your feminine side, and females will fall in love with your feather. This is a very funny and ironic nod to the act of peacocking!

9. Champagne signifies class. When combined with plastic handcuffs, the entire outfit is guaranteed to lead to an evening that no one, least of all the local news crews, will ever forget.

10. A red handkerchief is code for "Look at me—I'm different. I don't play by your everyday rules. Also, I'm kind of a rebel, so please disregard this neck pouch that holds my bus transfer and library card."

11. A blue handkerchief on the streets signifies that you will get shanked in a heartbeat. Inside a discotheque, however, a blue hanky tells a potential lover that you're up for practically anything, even shadow-dancing by yourself to Chris de Burgh's "Lady in Red." In fact, *especially* that.

Of course, if you don't have the confidence to peacock, or you simply left your wig and handcuffs at the gym, there's still one last route you can, as always, take. . . . Pity.

THE MALE PEACOCK: Our correction to God's mistake.

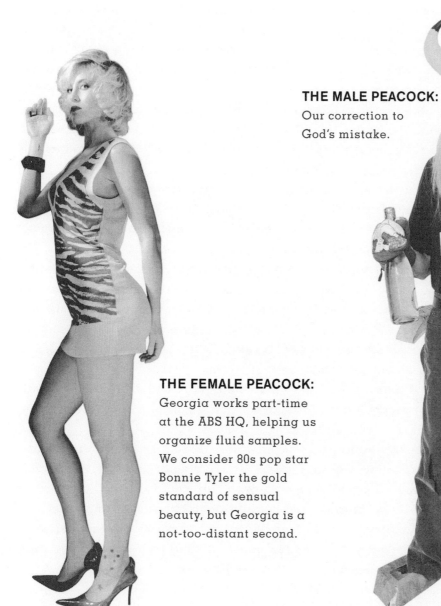

THE FEMALE PEACOCK: Georgia works part-time at the ABS HQ, helping us organize fluid samples. We consider 80s pop star Bonnie Tyler the gold standard of sensual beauty, but Georgia is a not-too-distant second.

DISCUSSING SEX AT WORK:

CAN'T A MAN COMPLIMENT A LADY'S DAMN CHEST THESE DAYS?

Every year, millions of employees attend mandatory seminars about sexual harassment in the workplace. While helpful at discouraging inappropriate sexual behavior, these seminars rarely educate us on what kinds of sexual activity or language *are* appropriate at work. Pretty unsexy, if you ask us.

Take this scenario. While alone in an elevator, a man asks his female co-worker if she has any tattoos in embarrassing places, and then informs her that she could be *"Maxim* hot" if only she lost five pounds and got hair extensions. Inappropriate, right?

Not so fast. What if the woman happens to be a longtime *Maxim* magazine subscriber and is disappointed that dress code regulations forbid her to show off the expensive new "serenity" tattoo over her coccyx? Or the Yosemite Sam tattoo close to her vagina, which reads C'MON OUT OF YOUR HOLE, VARMINT? In these cases, any comments from the man would be welcome indeed, and probably savored and recorded in a journal of sensual inspirations, like the one the authors strongly encourage you to keep (and currently available for purchase on our website, OurBodiesOurJunk.org, in two exciting colors: flesh and tomato red).

The ABS Sensual Inspirations Journal, available in two fabulous options!

Of course, it's also possible the woman will simply sue the man into poverty. But why not take a risk for once in your pathetic life, hypothetical man?

All of sexuality is about contrasts: masculine and feminine, hard and soft, the chilly atmosphere of a conference room and the warmth of someone whispering "Love your butt, Boo" into your ear during a PowerPoint presentation. Bear this in mind when bringing up the subject of sex at work, or anywhere similarly prudish (jury deliberation, as your baby's head is crowning, landing a plane whose pilot has just died of a heart attack, etc.).

Some guidelines:

- Double entendres are always fun (i.e., "Mmmph! I've got some *best practices* of my own I'd like to show you").
- Actually, you should never begin your double entendres with "Mmmph!"
- Never tickle a CEO. Or, for that matter, anyone sporting a belt buckle in the shape of a state.
- Bathroom fetishes are not an appropriate discussion topic at work, at least during lunch. They are best reserved for happy hour, when your audience is better suited to provide its full attention without all those workaday distractions.
- If your offer to take out a co-worker is declined, ask again, and then once more, but never an eighth time, unless it feels just right.
- Uninvited shoulder massages are a no-no. Uninvited scalp massages: a thrilling surprise.

As always in matters of sexuality, the number one rule for sex talk in the workplace is "Just Have Fun." After all, isn't fun what work is all about?

TEAM-BUILDING SEXERCISES FOR THE OFFICE

Interoffice "Elephant Line"

Team Bagging

Co-ed Naked Trust Falls

Sex with the Boss for a Raise

Coaxing the FedEx Courier into Anal

Choo-Choo Rides Round the Water Cooler

Pull My Rope and I'll Give You a Free Coffee Mug

Take This Knob and Shove It

RISKS AND REWARDS

It's axiomatic that the fish you catch and prepare yourself always tastes better than the one you find floating in a municipal garbage tank filled with rainwater. But did you ever wonder why? A fish is a fish, right? Well, not exactly. That's because the more work you put into a goal, the more you appreciate it. Just ask anyone who designed the pyramids.

Sex is no different. The more effort you put into acquiring it, the better it's going to be, as seen in this helpful guide:

OBSTACLES OVERCOME	SEXUAL SATISFACTION
Dragon, minotaur, or equivalent mythological beast	**EXCELLENT**
Seventh-generation blood feud between families	**VERY GOOD**
Deep suspicion of each other's Chinese zodiac signs	**GOOD**
Some ice on the roads, followed by more stairs than expected	**FAIR**
Zipper	**POOR**
Short wait in gang bang queue	**TERRIBLE**

OUR BODIES, OUR JUNK BEDITORIAL:
Creating Romance in a Clinical Setting

By Scott Jacobson, Urological Healing Professional

I made a solemn vow in med school: No matter how tough things got, I'd never take a job in which I couldn't wear my sarong to work. We make these promises to ourselves, and often we discard them, as I did in 1991, when taunts from hospital janitors began to distract me from my gynecological rounds. But the promise a medical professional makes to his patients is different. It is unbreakable. I'm speaking, of course, of the promise to comfort the patient. To do her no harm. And, above all, to make sure that her experience in your free clinic is as toe-curlingly, examination-table-slappingly erotic as possible.

How can I, as a respected, certified-at-one-point medical professional make such an unorthodox claim? Well, tell me something: Have you seen the movie Dr. T and the Women? Helen Hunt. Laura Dern. Tara Reid, at the very peak of her abilities. This motion picture embraces the notion that a patient can be titillated by the attentions of a handsome, wealthy gynecologist who is played by the late, great Richard Gere. I think this is a lesson that bears repeating.

Don't get me wrong—physicians in any specialty can be selfish and lazy. The doctors who are now reading this know what I mean:

- *"How can I intubate this esophagus quickly and just get on with it?"*
- *"Ugh, won't this bypass patient's sternum just spread already?"*
- *"Need the insurance number before I proceed."*

What kind of attitude is that? Slow it down! Luxuriate! Emergency medical care is not a race!

Before I continue, I should make this absolutely clear: I AM NOT TALKING ABOUT HAVING ACTUAL INTERCOURSE WITH PATIENTS! I'm talking about creating a mood, a state of mind. Did Dr. T actually have sex with his patients? Of course not! Although that might have made for an interesting plot development, and the movie's fans undoubtedly would have appreciated seeing how it all played out.

We can imagine it would have been confusing for Dr. T and his patient at first, both of them vibrating with an air of danger, as in any affaire de passion *frowned upon by conventional society. In the end it would have been replenishing both physically and spiritually, like a banquet meal after a weeklong cleanse, or a seasonal meditation sojourn at an ashram, or a half gram of cocaine. Perhaps Dr. T's colleagues would not understand, to say nothing of his wife, and don't get me started on the goons on the medical board—they'd eat Dr. T alive! Take his practice, his reputation, his house. They'd leave him with nothing but the sarong around his waist and a brand-new BMW with "I WILL CUT OFF YR NUTS PERV!!" etched in acid on the hood by a neighbor who read the story in the paper but didn't bother asking Dr. T for his side of it. And there's Dr. T, standing by the curb, hiding his tears behind Oakley-inspired sunglasses, while teenagers whip White Castle boxes at him from their vans and yell nasty comments about his ponytail. Idiots! All of them. Narrow-minded, hurtful idiots.*

Anyway.

I'm exceeding my allotted space for this Beditorial, so I'll sum up the remainder of my advice as succinctly as possible: incense, chemical hand warmers (by the crateload), diffuse crotch lighting, crepe waxing-table paper rather than the standard exam table variety (softer, durable, less rustling), frequent suggestions to rent Dr. T and the Women, peek-a-boo gowns, and above all else: respect, respect, respect!

HOW TO "MEET CUTE"

Before you rush out to meet the partner of your dreams, take a moment to lay some hot sexual groundwork.

Every year unhappy couples pour millions of dollars into the relationship therapy industry, and for what? True, nothing beats a healthy romantic relationship based on trust and communication, but of all the things that come close, making your friends and family falsely believe that you have a healthy relationship based on trust and communication is nothing to sneeze at.

The best way to do this is to have a repertoire of stories dealing with you and your partner, your continued desire to see each other's genitals despite knowing them better than your own toothbrush, your ability to make animated Disney couples look like that creepy couple in which the husband blinded his wife with lye, etc. But no relationship story is as reliably potent as the story of "how we met."

Too often couples leave their first meeting to chance, even though, statistically speaking, most chance encounters are mundane and would never impress imaginary future grandchildren or make your single friends feel like unlovable garbage. Like anything in a relationship, serendipity takes *work*. When you spot someone to whom you're physically attracted, don't rush into meeting or getting to know them. Take your time, follow and observe the person for a few weeks, and then plan your "meet cute."

ABS researchers have spent thousands of hours reviewing highly romantic footage of Andie MacDowell, Billy Crystal, John Corbett, and other "meet cute" experts, and have come to a few conclusions.

The following meetings rate as successfully "cute":

- A cocky man at a bowling alley bowls a strike. As he dances in celebration, the bowling ball somehow ricochets back into his testicles, knocking him into the arms of a passing woman who will be his soul mate, then his ex-wife, and then his wife again.

One particularly effective "meet cute" requires the mechanical sabotage of a merry-go-round.

- A sad young gal rides a merry-go-round alone. Due to a mechanical malfunction, the carousel begins to spin wildly out of control and the woman is thrown from her wooden horse into the arms of a passing man who will soon become not only her soul mate but also her hospice nurse. (Note: In practice, this would require some mechanical sabotage of said merry-go-round. Proceed with a certain degree of caution.)

- A no-nonsense career woman breaks a heel and tumbles ass-first into a garbage can. As she wriggles her arms and legs comically, she's spotted by a handsome working-class man who happens to be doing some high-end construction in her loft and has been dressed down by the client for getting sawdust on her expensive hand-woven Persian kilim rug. "Well, what have we here? Maybe this 'big, dumb lummox' is good for *something* after all," says the man with a cocky grin and a complicit wink, gently taunting the uppity woman before agreeing to pull her out of the garbage can—but only *if* she grants him a deep kiss and a quick slippity-slap. Not to mention $100 in cash for his trouble.

Some more "meet cute" scenarios:

- Him, a part-time bartender with dreams of the big time. Her, a drug lord's wife, half in the bag and looking for some fun.
- Her, going into labor in the back of a cab. Him, a germophobic cabby sporting his Wednesday whites.
- Him, running wildly from the bulls in Pamplona. Her, blindfolded and unknowingly separated from her trust group.

- Him, prepped and awaiting his first-ever colonic.
  Her, picking the wrong door for her herbal wrap.

Getting the idea? If so, it's time to begin the meticulous process of planning to meet your future soul mate!*

But first, let's try to spruce up your appearance.

GUILT-TRIPPING:
SEDUCTION'S HANDICAPPED COUSIN

Some are discouraged by what they see as the cruel, Darwinist reality of human sexual attraction. It's true that when someone sizes up a potential mate, he or she is actually on the lookout for qualities that could be duplicated in an offspring. That might mean traits such as physical strength, natural beauty, and evidence of emotional stability. But let's not forget, babies also need constant affection, cry a lot for absolutely no reason, and spend most of the day on their backs staring blankly at the ceiling. Perhaps you possess some valuable baby traits after all.

As a tool of seduction, being aware of one's utter unfitness for life on this planet can come in handy. Sure, many seducers follow the model of Lord Byron, legendary ladies' man and author of *Don Juan*. But also nearly as influential was Byron's nineteenth-century contemporary Sir Thomas Swoonsworthy, and his "Ode to M'Lady's Cheeks Most Wond'rous Fair":

Oh m'lady! That a wretch such as I—
Gaunt of face
Concave of chest
Tubercular of lung
Pimpled of buttock
Hacking with a cough most conversationally disruptive
Dwarfish in stature

*ABS cannot be held responsible if your "meet cute" results in serious injury, legal action, arrest, or death for one or both parties.

Okay, Lord Byron, we get it. You got tons of trim.

Unappealing of dentition
Unreliable of bowel
Gruesomely form'd of penis
Needy of hugs e'er ill-timed
Hairless head to toe—
That e'en I, m'lady, shall be allowed to gaze upon your cheeks—
'Tis a wondrous blessing
E'en if you already have a boyfriend . . .
And I a skunk pelt for a hat.

Sir Thomas Swoonsworthy in better days

Sir Swoonsworthy's eloquence so affected the gentler sex of the day that women would often let things proceed much further than they would have had he not been so utterly nonthreatening and gay-acting.

If you too are interested in using guilt to your sexual advantage, first bear in mind that whatever sex you manage to elicit from your partner will be awkward, uncomfortable, and borderline traumatic for both of you. Knowing this in advance will give you the proper level of hopelessness needed for your guilt trip to work.

Then, once you are out on a dinner date—most likely with a friend of a friend who has only been told, "He's such a sweetheart, and you both love urban musicals"—you must lay the foundation for your guilt trip with a grand romantic gesture. This can be as simple as an inappropriately large teddy-bear bouquet presented with a five-to-ten-second kiss on the forehead, or it can be as involved as a reenactment of the screaming-into-the-abyss scene from *Garden State* with you as Zach Braff, a waitress as Natalie Portman, and a busboy dragged in as Peter Sarsgaard.

Now that you have gone out of your way to express your desire for sex, you're free to sit back for the remainder of the date and be a "nice guy," i.e., the type of person who doesn't play "head games" such as flirting or pretending to be interested in what the other person has to say when all you really want is to discuss the uncomfortable side effects of this new antidepressant from Mexico you're giving a shot.

By the time the check arrives, if your date doesn't want sex with you, it's probably because she does not like nice guys. The moment you sense intercourse is not in the works, convey displeasure by limiting your verbal responses to monotone phrases like "Cool... mmm-hmm... yeah." Allow for long, awkward pauses between comments. This will allow your date the opportunity to remember how little is going on later that night, and give her a chance to eagerly conclude, *Why the hell not—if it'll put a cork in all his sad-sack groaning, let's just do it already. Jesus!*

Important: If your date chooses to not have sex with you after all, don't take it as a sign you're doing something wrong! Remind yourself that even though Mother Nature's system of human courtship has produced a world population of nearly seven billion, if a great guy like you still finds it impossible to mate, perhaps Mother Nature is—let's just admit it—nothing more than an embittered lesbian.

HEY, DIDJA KNOW...

The male sex pheromone is most closely replicated by the scent of a spicy-chicken sandwich from Wendy's?

The larger the gap between a person's eyes, the greater the odds of them not attending prom?

Since 1964, there have been seven documented cases of women impregnated by water slides?

Successfully coaxing a prostitute into allowing you to tickle her anus for an extra $5 is technically considered "wooing"?

Soft kissing is a natural diuretic?

Research shows that the most effective online-dating photo is of a man weeping with joy over a litter of still-wet newborn squirrels?

Up until 1953, a good long stare was considered "getting to second base"?

A male's sexual availability is often signaled by a fresh dot of pre-ejaculate staining his Dockers?

CHAPTER 3

FOREPLAY

PENETRATION'S

WAITING ROOM

If you had just survived the sinking of the *Titanic* and found yourself on a lifeboat with room for only two chapters from this book, which two would you let on board?

Allow us, the authors, to submit a choice of our own: this one. Also, the next one.

That's because foreplay and intercourse constitute most of what we now consider sexual activity. For many years, these elements of sexuality were marginalized. All too common were intimacy guides that characterized a sexual encounter as an event in which two people made flirtatious eye contact only to then retreat to separate attics to masturbate and pray. These days, of course, foreplay and intercourse have been thoroughly mainstreamed, and the majority of us can't believe that there ever was a time when it would have been inappropriate to own a coffee mug with I HATE MONDAYS BUT NOT THE THRILLING MUSK OF MY LADY'S VAGINA on it.

Before foreplay and intercourse were popularized,
this item would have been unthinkable.

We tend to think of foreplay in terms of physical but non-penetrative acts such as oral sex or spinal manipulation. But *anything* preceding sex that revs up the libido can be considered foreplay—a decadent meal, a bubble bath, a kill shot at the pistol range. In fact, when you view foreplay in its broadest sense, it isn't always possible to tell when "sex" has officially begun. For example, is the couple next to you getting an estimate for a new transmission, or are they engaged in an elaborate, erotic prologue that will take them through a trip to the dry cleaners, a friend's barbecue, armpit worship, a smattering of butt stuff, and then ultimately intercourse? It's impossible to know without inquiring, so don't be shy about it. Fact: 79 percent of couples buying a file cabinet at Walmart are just itching to be asked what, in particular, gets them off.

If foreplay is the warm-up band, then intercourse is the headlining act, the culmination of years of romantic pursuit or two Long Island iced teas. The basics are as follows: The man inserts his erect penis into a woman's vagina. The couple need not love each other very much, as your parents claimed, nor even keep it a "special secret," the way your PE coach once told you.

However, the basics aren't enough. To become the kind of lover your curriculum vitae and professional references already suggest you are, you need this chapter. And the next.

First, some necessary background.

THE HUMAN SEXUAL-RESPONSE CYCLE:
THE FOUR SEASONS OF HORNY

Traditionally, the phases of the human sexual-response cycle are subdivided into four parts: excitement, plateau, orgasm, and recovery. It's a bit of an oversimplification, but you can think of them as the four seasons of sex.

1. SPRING/EXCITEMENT (MARCH 20–JUNE 21)

- House cleaned top to bottom.
- Quickening of breath, increase in blood pressure, engorging of the muscles, scary beast-like look in the eyes, rapid change in skin tone, spontaneous splitting of shirts and pants.
- Nipples (if present) stiffen.

2. SUMMER/PLATEAU (JUNE 22–SEPTEMBER 21)

- Fourth of July spent on Cape Cod.
- Genital lubrication can get really out of hand.
- Clitoris, ever the optimist, grows extremely sensitive.

3. AUTUMN/ORGASM (SEPTEMBER 22–DECEMBER 20)

- Wheat harvested.
- Brief but intensely pleasurable period of furious genital spasming. Basically feels like eating a really good double-fudge brownie. In men, this results in the expulsion of semen into a heart-shaped hanky or onto a *Ladies of Sam's Club* wall calendar. In women, the orgasm is reportedly many times more intense and many times less disgusting. If you believe the legends, the female orgasm can be detected by the faint scent of candy apples and the sudden appearance of a white dove.

4. WINTER/RESOLUTION (DECEMBER 21–MARCH 19)

- Snowboarding given a try.
- Physiological heightening eases, and a period of recovery ensues. In some females, however, this period is brief, and they can quickly reenter the sexual-response cycle; the recovery period for men is generally longer and is spent waiting for a

canister of Pringles to materialize out of thin air. In addition, some men experience a certain type of cognitive amplification, during which they suddenly recall that "thing" they have to do immediately.

- Heartbeat slows, muscles relax. High fives are exchanged. If bets have been placed, it is customary to settle them at this time. Congratulations are in order. You just did sex!

Of course, just as an astronomer's model of the solar system doesn't quite correspond with our everyday interactions with Jupiter, the medical establishment's four-stage response cycle doesn't quite align with what we experience between the sheets, now does it?

A new and more relevant template is required, one that every-one can use to monitor their own sexual progression.

THE HUMAN-SEXUAL RESPONSE CYCLE (REVISED)

1. Wake up in a cold sweat
2. Breakfast at Pancake Johnny's
3. Excitement
4. Hannity on the drive home
5. Pet chinchilla blindfolded
6. Find yourself a sex mate
7. Greet sex mate
8. Lick the first 1,000 numbers of pi "down there"
9. Plateau
10. Light snack
11. A sip of a fine cocktail
12. Search online for jobs not requiring any references
13. Fill out tax forms
14. Play with the chinchilla
15. Become a fan of "Sex" on Facebook
16. Practice lute

17. Use prison code to tap out "I think I love you" on your lover's vitals
18. Thirty to fifty minutes of intense physical bliss and ecstatic contact with the unknown—you are a bright shiny whistle alive with the breath of God*
19. Orgasm
20. Flex time
21. Hand bus fare to sex mate
22. Disentanglement from drift net
23. Recovery
24. Lingering trauma
25. Quick snooze
26. Wake up in a cold sweat
27. Blindfold removed from pet chinchilla

KISSING:
LOVEMAKING'S OPENING SALVO

For most couples, kissing is the first intimate contact that crosses the line into true romantic sexual touch (the majority of authorities agree that frottage in a jam-packed food court does not count). Some simple but often overlooked things to remember about the act of kissing:

- Mouth toys are unnecessary. Piercings, fake vampire teeth, corncob pipes, and whistles aren't kissing-party favors, but merely hurdles on the way to rapture. When it comes to kissing and the mouth, the ABS motto is KISS (Keep It Simple, Stupid!).

*Phase has been observed only in Darius, the sinewy man in our Bikram yoga class with the ass-length rattail. Hey, Darius!

Although incredibly fun, mouth toys can make kissing difficult.

- The mouth is sensitive. Touch memory lingers on the lips and tongue. It's best not to bite, tongue-thwack, or play tag with your partner's mouth parts. If you must do any of these, first try numbing your partner's tongue and uvula with a topical anesthetic.
- The nose is the mouth's cranky upstairs neighbor. If your mouth tastes like a peanut-butter-and-Doritos sandwich, just imagine what it smells like to your partner! Either brush your teeth before kissing or discreetly introduce a second peanut-butter-and-Doritos sandwich into your partner's mouth, to effectively cancel out your own odors.

SENSUOUS TOUCH:
THE BASICS

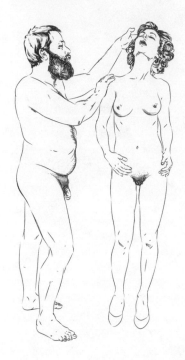

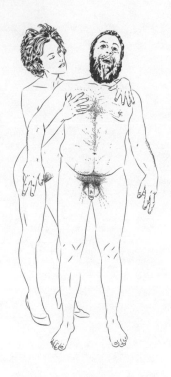

SENSUOUS FINGER COMB

Move your hand slowly toward your partner's face. Find his or her hairline and gently begin combing your hand through the hair while simultaneously tapping the scalp with your thumb. Avoid inserting a finger into the ear (that's a separate touch altogether). If stymied by tangles, distract your partner with a gentle puff of air to the face as you force your hand through the obstructing hair mass. If your partner is bald or wearing a swimming cap, pretend not to notice and proceed anyway.

BREAST TOUCH

When it comes to the breasts, light, manual stimulation can be extremely erotic. As can heavy tickling. (Note: When initiating a tickle, smile a lot and giggle loudly, as a way of conveying to your partner, "This is fun! This is play! This is life as it *should* be!")

LI'L PUMPKIN EATER

Many women report finding the sensation of a gentle nib-nib-nibbling at the back of the head to be sexually stimulating, especially if performed while crouching on Easter-basket grass.

GRUN-GRUN TOUCH

This custom touch, developed at ABS for your use and pleasure, involves working your hands over your recumbent partner's body in a fluttering manner, all the while whispering, "Grun-grun-grun-grun-grun-grun-grun." Repeat. If your partner awakes with a start or stares at you in disbelief, you can clear up the confusion by saying, "Chill out, it's only me," and then gracefully segue into a full-body massage.

THE EYES: SEMAPHORES OF INTERCOURSE

Whether we realize it or not, we communicate through nonverbal cues, most of which are transmitted through our facial features. Although our nostrils flare when we're angry and our ears withdraw completely into our skulls when we're sad, nothing on our face communicates our innermost thoughts quite like the eyes. The pupils, in particular, are well attuned to our level of arousal, and it's widely understood that dilated pupils indicate that a person is primed for sexual activity.*

ABS cross-cultural research has identified five universal dilation states that convey much finer messages.

"I'm hoping to have intercourse with your left half."

"I want you, but I've drunk far too much backwoods hooch to properly express myself."

"I'm very aroused. I've just forgotten how to dilate."

"No matter what I say, I will just use you for your free waffles and then kick you to the curb."

"I'm preoccupied with tomorrow's PowerPoint presentation."

*Can also indicate that someone has lowered the blinds slightly.

DRY HUMPING:
THE ROUGH BALLET

Here's a fun experiment to try at home: take two chalkboard-eraser-size blocks of wood and affix a swatch of denim to one side of each. If you rub these blocks together quickly and vigorously, you will smell sweet, hot denim, an invigorating aroma that wends its way into the memory banks of anyone who has ever been in the throes of a particularly rambunctious session of outside-of-the-clothes heavy petting, dry slidin', or hobo humpin'.

Simulate dry humping by rubbing wooden blocks together.

After thirty minutes of frenzied friction, you and your partner will take off together, soaring madly through a lusty airstream, powered by a high-powered crotch-to-crotch piston-pumping engine.

Sixty minutes later your arms will be tired, and the sweat will have long since pooled on your brow, but when the one-hour mark passes—your grip on the blocks now cramping your hands, the denim threadbare, gentle wisps of piquant jean smoke suffusing the air—your mind will race back to your very first magical dry hump. Sophomore year. On a pile of camo netting in your Uncle Rick's duck blind. The cramped space spilling over with that dank, musky scent of partially fulfilled lust. The violent motions of your clothing-inhibited sex rite, filled with equal parts wonderful anger and irritated love. The smell of old banana peels.

Back to the present: You finally collapse, one of your hands completely numb, the other throbbing. Perfect, no? A faultless metaphor, this, for the two body parts that tango most sweetly in that delicate, unforgettable dance we often call . . . the "finished-basement bang-bang."

CUNNILINGUS:
ORAL MANEUVERS IN THE DARK

Now for the nitty-gritty . . .

It used to be that sexual pleasure was the domain of men alone—if it felt good, it was a penis feeling it. In a typical lovemaking session of the 1950s, a man would push his member through the slit in his pajama bottoms, mechanically thrust for a few minutes, run pomade through his hair, read the paper, ejaculate, pat wifey on the head, and fall asleep. But as the second half of the twentieth century unfolded, women were entering the workforce and worrying about their needs in record numbers. Women who had squatted over mirrors fully clothed were now doing so in the nude, beholding the glory of their exposed genitalia for the very first time. The message to men was clear: *Satisfy us, or we'll find a butterfly-shaped sex toy that will.*

The problem early on was that many women knew their bodies only slightly better than their wholly ignorant partners did, guiding them with instructions such as "Go left—no, right, *right*" or "There should be a lever here *somewhere*." But even in these better-educated times, pleasuring a woman is more complicated than doing likewise for a man because the vagina is intrinsically much more complex. It's the difference between assembling a thousand-piece jigsaw puzzle and shoving a fat kid's face into a public toilet. But it *can* be done.

Chapter 1 of this book has already discussed the vagina generally, so if you haven't already memorized it all, or at least the coolest parts, you should do so now. Please keep the following in mind: Even though a lot of vaginas share similar construction, each and every woman experiences pleasure somewhat differently. Some women have a clitoris that's so sensitive, even a grazing touch is almost unbearable; other women need their clits worked like a speed bag. How do you know which you're dealing with? Communication. You can learn all the ludicrous "tricks" you want, but none will take you further than:

- "How does this feel?"
- "Do you like what my hand is doing? In sign language, it's the word for 'vulture.'"

Cunnilingus is the Rubik's Cube you must solve with your tongue in order to keep your girlfriend from leaving you.

Tricks will only get you so far. Don't just assume this man is an expert at eating pussy.

- "As I scoop jelly beans into this jar, I want you to stop me when the exact amount accurately reflects your level of satisfaction with my most recent touch."
- "If that last nibble were a Marine, what rank would you give it? Private, private first class, lance corporal, corporal, sergeant, staff sergeant, gunnery sergeant, master sergeant, first sergeant, master gunnery sergeant, sergeant major, sergeant major of the Marine Corps, warrant officer 1, chief warrant officer 2, chief warrant officer 3, chief warrant officer 4, chief warrant officer 5, second lieutenant, first lieutenant, captain, major, lieutenant colonel, colonel, brigadier general, major general, lieutenant general, or general?"

Of course, your questions will amount to nothing if you're not paying attention to the answers. And sometimes these answers will not be offered in the form of clean and neat sentences—especially if she's enjoying herself! In the throes of passion, a woman might very easily confuse *prescribe* and *proscribe* or misapply the subjunctive, and it's up to you, her lover, to work with whatever grammatical construction you are given.

But don't forget: even with wonderful dialogue between you and your partner, it's sometimes fun to throw in something unexpected. Like a chef who adds a dash of Adderall to his marinara sauce, you can surprise your partner with a couple of moves she's never seen before (unless she's been orally pleasured by an ABS researcher in the past). Remember to take your time before diving in! Work your way down to her breasts and stomach with soft kisses, bypassing her vulva for an agonizing moment to smooch one inner thigh, then the other, unless you hate the other one for some reason, in which case skip it. Now advance to her mound. Inhale deeply, letting her know that her aroma does not bother you at all. You can even whisper, "Your scent turns me on," or something simpler, such as: "Your bouquet drives me wild. I'd bottle and distribute it, if I could ever get the start-up capital. Unfortunately, the banks just aren't lending these days, which is ridiculous. Why did we pump in those billions of taxpayer dollars? So that they could just sit on a big pile of cash? You know?"

By now, your partner should be more than ready for your oral attentions. She's bucking her hips and pulling your head toward her madly lubricated pudenda. This might seem like a perfect opportunity to leave the room and cultivate a new hobby, but actually it's showtime.

With your tongue dabbing the opening to her vagina and your finger tickling her clitoral hood—no, no, other way around. Tongue, clit. Finger, vaginal opening. Anyway, now cram—no, gently *insert*, not cram—your finger inside. But before you do that, you should have already . . . so, with your *second* finger . . . anus ever so lightly . . . with your tongue splayed into the shape of the NASA logo, you can . . . pretty much any woodwind instrument . . . some more nibbling and—*Damn it to hell!* Sorry! We haven't done this in a long, long while. The eventual Kindle version will contain the answer.

Anyway, when she asks you where you learned such an astonishing maneuver, don't worry! We'll never tell!

FELLATIO:
WOMEN CAN GIVE ORAL SEX, TOO!

The vagina was designed to be the ultimate reproductive incentive for men: Why, yes, you *could* penetrate that hollowed-out squash or that crevice in a rock wall, but wouldn't you rather enter someplace warm and snug and altogether human, a body cavity with the pleasurable extraction of your semen incorporated into its very design? The answer for many men is *absolutely*, just as soon as their organ has been worked over for ten minutes orally. For these men, any sexual encounter that doesn't at some point involve the orifice where pizza is chewed is erotically incomplete. In fact, a few men prefer it almost exclusively, and their frustrated partners are left to coax vaginal penetration using a variety of elaborate disguises.

By contrast, some women are squeamish about giving oral sex. They think it's dirty, for one thing. Sadly, this is a myth that owes its longevity to the fact that fellatio was first popularized in the nine-

Partners of men who strongly favor oral sex sometimes resort to disguising their vagina as a mouth.

teenth century by Pennsylvania coal miners. The truth is that as long as a man demonstrates some attention to hygiene—grooming, washing, occasional polishing—the average penis is no less sanitary than a favorite ear of corn a hobo might keep under his hat. But if cleanliness is an issue, there are certainly ways to address it.

First of all, rare is the man who likes being told that his genitals are distressingly filthy, so if you *must* bring up the subject, take your partner's feelings into consideration. Instead of baldly stating that his privates remind you of something you once saw in the zoo's ape habitat, smile widely and blow a kiss toward the penis. Without any mention of the baffling grass stains along his shaft, tell your partner *before* you actually begin performing oral sex that you'd like to tease him with janitorial supplies, such as a wire scrub brush and a diluted ammonia solution. With this approach, you'll keep your partner happy while still receiving the blissful satisfaction of avoiding typhus.

A coat of arms can transform a common penis into the most noble organ in the realm.

Of course, a clean peen may not be enough for you. Another issue women struggle with is the notion that fellatio is somehow improper—and maybe it *does* seem a bit unladylike to take a man's penis into one's mouth, even if the organ is classed up with euphemisms such as "sperm musket" or "denture duster." But if you won't debase yourself, you can take the opposite tack and elevate the stature of your partner's member. If you have the wherewithal, award it an honorary degree from Emory University; otherwise, work with your partner on other ways to ennoble his penis. For example, design an august coat of arms for it, or assign it one of the nation's more prestigious area codes. At the very least, have your partner lay his genitals on some piano keys and imagine you're beholding a virtuoso at work.

Okay, now you're ready and willing to orally satisfy your partner. Oh, but *how*? Should you suck it like a straw? Blow on it like a birthday candle? Pinch it with your teeth and yank forcefully on it like a puppy might do with a bag of potato chips? Similar to the vagina, each and every penis is different, a one-of-a-kind snowflake that can impregnate you. As always, communication and listening are key. If your partner *mmmmmm*s with pleasure, whatever you're doing, keep doing it! If he winces, withdraws, or falsely confesses to being an Al Qaeda operative, perhaps you're being too aggressive. Keeping those general guidelines in mind, you can also add the following techniques to your repertoire.

The Water Slide

Beginning at the tip of the penis, slowly guide your tongue down and around the shaft until your "slide" reaches the bottom. Then, with sporadic sighs of impatience and gripes about how crowded it is, climb the penis for at least half an hour until your "line" finally gets back to the top. Repeat until exhausted and ready to walk home.

Approaching the Lighthouse

If your partner likes a little teasing, he's sure to adore this. Attach a standard appliance lightbulb to the tip of the penis and work your way toward it from across the darkened room, as if a ship in search of safe harbor. Add some drama to the role-play by rubbing your cheek against your partner's thigh and making grinding noises as if your mouth vessel has momentarily run aground.

The Koala

Clamp your arms and legs around the shaft and alternately lick and gently nibble the head as you would a eucalyptus leaf. This technique is easier to execute with longer, sturdier penises, so only attempt this if you're supremely confident in your partner's measurements (10 to 20 inches is a safe starting point).

A Whittle Stick for Gramma

Pretend you are Gramma, a feisty old dame searching through the undergrowth (the pubic region) for that perfect edible mushroom (a man's pleasure center). Once you locate it, use that old metal detector (your tongue) from the Korean War (summers on the Virginia Shore) to find what you really came here for: his penis (his penis).

THE SEMEN TASTE CHALLENGE

There has always been an elephant in the room when the subject of oral sex is discussed, and that elephant tastes like semen. The undesirable flavor of semen can present an obstacle in a couple's otherwise healthy sex life. But what can be done about it? Presenting the semen in a fancy snifter doesn't seem to help, and neither does dissolving a sugar cube in a tall glass of ejaculate. Is there *nothing* that can be done?

Believe it or not, there is. It's been scientifically proven (in a lab!) that there exists a direct correlative between diet and the taste and odor of semen. Consuming the proper type of food thirty minutes before lovemaking can make the difference between a bitter aftertaste and a bitter and sour aftertaste.

IF YOU CONSUME A . . .	YOUR SEMEN WILL TASTE LIKE . . .
Six-inch Subway Roast Beef Sandwich	A Six-inch Quiznos Honey Bacon Sub
Granny Smith apple	A canvas sack filled with fresh muskrat hides
Glass of white zinfandel	The ashtray at an AA meeting
A plate of raw oysters	Baked clams*
Can of consommé	A discarded homemade diaper
Pair of shoelaces	Big League Chew (grape)
Bottle of carpet shampoo	Calvin Klein's CK One for Men and Women
Fun-size Snickers bar	Taco meat served out of a park ranger's mitten
Teaspoon of your own semen	Six-inch Subway Roast Beef Sandwich

*If taking antidepressants, this flavor will sometimes be identified as any one of the following: Tropical Pineapple, Little Italy Pizza, Deli Horseradish, Honduran Banana, Garlic Knot, Just-Off-the-Highway Cinnamon Buns, Sudanese Kumquat, Salty Knoblewurst, Zesty Dipping Sauce, or Rose Water found in an Extra-Fancy Lavatory.

One final note on fellatio: As of 1987, the most recent year for which data were available, more than one in three women, across racial and socioeconomic lines, indicated that they "often" or "very often" forgot the scrotum, while fewer than one in twenty-five described kneading, tickling, or tongue-bathing the testicles as an "indispensable component of blow-job protocol." It will be interesting to see what effect recent ABS outreach efforts—speaking engagements at women's colleges, haranguing launderette patrons, sponsoring a float in Boston's next St. Patrick's Day parade—will have on these statistics.

DIDDLIN' THE HUMPHRIES
(AND OTHER ORAL SEXTRAS)

Oral sex isn't all about your mouth going south. There are a number of other options you can use to make that jaunt down to Mexico a whole lot spicier, and many of them are cheaper than a one-way bus ticket to "Listerine-ville"!

TIPS FOR MEN

Wig out, dude

Women love something to hold on to while they're experiencing mouth love, and 89 percent of the time they'll grab a man's hair like it's the yoke of a rocket ship they're steering into hyperspace. Make it interesting for her! Keep a nice selection of luxurious wigs on hand. Especially good choices are faux pompadours, psychedelic cornrows, and the lustrous Johnny Winter "white tiger."

Fingerless gloves

Every woman loves fingerless gloves because they bring to mind cool biker types and professional bowlers. When you're performing oral sex and wearing these, it's the best of all worlds—the feel and fragrance of leather, fingers free to poke and prod, and attitude to spare. Get some.

Invisible bongos

Unleash your hidden percussionist, gents. While your mouth and tongue are doing the blue-collar work on your partner, place your hands on her belly and let the rhythm command you. Be it "Turkey in the Straw" or a funky percussive tribute to the late, great Bob Weir's global-music project "Planet Drum," this extra contact will, in no time, have your lady sky-dancing in another dimension of ecstasy.

TIPS FOR WOMEN

Snack attack

Ladies, does your man love snacking? That's not a euphemism: Does he love chips, cake, yummy cookies, and the like? If so, get ready to blow his penis *and* his taste buds! We recommend wearing a snakeskin pouch filled to the brim with various sweets and treats, for just that right dash of kink. While you're performing wonderful oral love on your man, gently reach up and insert some tasty nibbles into his mouth in the manner of hand-feeding a raccoon.

Diddlin' the Humphries

A man's testicles are like his two ugliest friends. They're around him constantly and they get no love elsewhere. Your man's joy will only increase a hundredfold if you show these two losers a bit of attention. Anything will do, even a slight nod or a casual "Hey, how's it goin'?"

EATING AIN'T CHEATING: FACT OR EXQUISITE FANTASY?

Jeffy, age 37, writes:

I've been married eight years. Two beautiful kids, a house. The last thing in the world I would do is cheat. The other night the wife and I were going to catch *Spamalot* down at the Civic Center for our tenth anniversary, so we had over Josie, the nineteen-year-old babysitter. My wife was in the kids' room saying her goodbyes, and Josie and I were alone. We figured, what the hey? Eating ain't cheating. Josie and I engaged in five or six minutes of intense, mutually satisfying cunnilingus on the living room ottoman, until my wife walked in. I have to say, Josie and I were both *very* surprised by my wife's reaction. Negative! Just plain angry. We reminded her of the phrase.

Did the man deserve his wife's vitriol? Probably not. We're taught from a young age that things that rhyme are true. Think "A stitch in time saves nine" or "Beef burrito make gringo go loco." That's why it can be frightening and confusing when a phrase rhymes perfectly—indeed, when the words fit together with the laser-cut syntactical precision of the almighty word of God—and yet the sentiment could possibly (we still don't know for sure) be flawed. Perhaps the concept of sexual fidelity *does* bar the placing of a stranger's genitals in one's mouth for the purpose of inducing an orgasm. Perhaps not. Romance needs its mysteries.

DISCUSSING ORAL SEX WITH YOUR CHILDREN

Sex is a lot like chess. It is easy to learn and yet impossible to master, and it should never be performed with a Russian in a public park. In other words, if sex is confusing to practically everyone, you can only imagine how confusing it can be for your child! We here at ABS *do not* recommend talking with your son or daughter about sex until they hit eighteen years old, as this is the law and there is nothing we can do about it, except to continue to picket outside the Supreme Court every morning before work.

With that said, if you must teach your children about sexuality (hint, hint), please approach it *gently*. As any parent can tell you there is something sublime in the moment your child first bounds toward you with that uncertain bowlegged wobble, throws his arms around your legs, stares up at you with those warm pools of innocence we call eyes, and asks, "Pa, what is cunnilingus?"

Discussing oral sex with your child can seem frustratingly complex. Sadly, it's never as simple as placing your child at your knee and telling him, "When a bee loves a bird very much, he uses his proboscis to trace the alphabet around the bird's engorged cloaca."

Fortunately, there are some excellent sources to help navigate parents through the tricky subject of explaining oral sex to their children. These supplemental materials were produced by experts in the field of child development, and each will earn the official ABS "Seal of Arousal," just after the check properly clears.

THE DING-A-LINGS SING-ALONG SERIES PRESENTS "THE WACKITY FLAPPITY WORLD OF ORAL PLEASURE"

Before the members of this popular children's musical group were discovered murdered on the outskirts of a New Jersey gypsy encampment, they released a delightful collection of sing-alongs about the carnal arts.

Songs such as "Six and Nine Makes Jolly Time" and "Why the Blackbird Won't Go Down" prove infectiously catchy while also treating their exquisitely sensitive subject matter with the gentleness it deserves—as evidenced by this lyrical excerpt from "Doggy Honks the Horn (The Clitoris Song)":

> *Doggy honks the horn*
> *Kitty rides the bus*
> *Daddy puts his mouth*
> *on Mommy's clitoris*

> *[Jazzy solo]*

> *Farmer's in the barn*
> *Turtle's in the sand*
> *Mommy's tongue dances*
> *over Daddy's swollen glans*

> *[Rapturous applause]*

ORAL TRADITIONS® CUNNILINGUS AND FELLATIO ROLE-PLAY FINGER PUPPETS

Safe, nontoxic, and made from 100% recycled tires, these unique finger puppets were designed to help parents share with their children even the most complicated nuances of giving and receiving oral pleasure, all in a way that's fun and easy to remember.

The set includes three finger puppets and several colorful playsets—including "Farm House" and "Parking Garage."

THE BIG O, OR THE ORGASM:
THE EVER-PRESENT ELUSIVE MALE ORGASM AND THE MYTH OF THE FEMALE ORGASM

It just occurred to us that we've failed to discuss in detail the most important aspect of all sexual play: the orgasm! Love it or hate it, the orgasm has the distinction of being one of the few events less subtle than the simultaneous discharge of sixty flamethrowers.* From the bedsheets of easily embarrassed twelve-year-old Nate Quinn of Coral Springs, Florida, to the Oval Office itself, the propulsive expulsion of semen has left its indelible mark. It's a tangible thing, this spontaneous work of eruptive art you point to and say, "I created this," and it's no surprise that so many disillusioned men have left their spiritually unfulfilling service-sector jobs to masturbate full-time.

Then there's the female, ahem, orgasm. Sure, sex is pleasurable for women, but in the manner of a pedicure or a new and surprising soft cheese. True shuddering, galaxy-traversing ecstasy belongs to men and men alone. While billions of women have reported achieving orgasm, these are just billions of subjective experiences—sometimes multiple subjective experiences clustered one after another along with ecstatic howling. Tellingly, when our U-Haul van pulls up to a woman to take post-coital vaginal-dilation measurements, the attitude is "Stay back, or I'll call the cops." As anyone with intelligence knows, this tactic is the last refuge of someone who's losing an argument.

If you're a man, try to understand your partner's anguish and rein in your satisfaction. After climaxing—in mid-climax, if possible—

*See *State of Maryland v. ABS* for more details.

yawn, shrug, or absentmindedly flick a silverfish off the bed frame. If you're a woman, take some consolation in the fact that while your partner may be the only one who can experience an orgasm, you're the only one who can get pregnant from it.

FIRSTHAND ACCOUNTS OF THE ALLEGED FEMALE "ORGASM"

Roger, age 33:

"I picked up this Wiccan girl in Duluth and we went to an Outback Steakhouse. Afterward we were getting busy in my truck. I touched her down there, between her legs, and . . . you ever toss a wildcat in a pond for kicks? This girl rose up in the air like that seat was electrified! She scratched my face, screamed, 'Feets don't fail me now!' and disappeared in a puff of smoke. I thought it was just some witchy shit, but now I know she orgasmed. Fantastic!"

Cody, age 20:

"It was my first time, but not hers. She was my best friend's aunt, Rhonda, and she was like thirty at the time. Don't say nothing, please. I was on top of her, doing it, and she begin to breathe real differently, almost like she was wheezing or something. Then suddenly her legs curled around my back real tight and she grabs my ass and pulled me toward her. I thought she was having a seizure. It scared the shit out of me. I panicked and threw up. Right then Stevie Wonder's 'Don't Drive Drunk' from the *Lady in Red* soundtrack came on the radio. After that, the night was kind of a bust."

Cap'n Reese, age 101:

"The ladies arch their back and the fireworks goes off. Then you feel a dull pain at the back of your skull and when you regain consciousness—boom!—you're in the Navy."

Understanding Sexual Afflictions

By Mike Sacks, Sexual Dysfunction Life Coach

Anoxgasmi: The Inability to Orgasm in Front of a Paying Crowd

Last fall, as we do every year, ABS threw its annual Picnic and Festivity Day on the South Lawn of the White House. While this is technically illegal, we never seem to be bothered by police or government authorities, most likely because we make a really big show out of also inviting the mentally challenged children of our secretarial staff.

Favorite activities include three-legged races, egg tosses, and watching strangers having sex on tumbling mats as we eat from large buckets of kettle corn and sip from homemade buck brew that one of our board members whips up whenever he's not incarcerated or traveling around Canada as the house sexpert for Cirque du Soleil. (For the record, attendees who don't pay the $150 special fornication fee are not allowed to watch from inside the Titillation Tent—they are only allowed to watch from a few yards away, next to the giant TV monitors and falafel stands.)

In 2005, Johnny Fortress (real name) volunteered to participate in this very special rite of passage we force upon all of our temps. Seemingly healthy, Johnny just adored sex, but when it came time for the big day, he was unable to orgasm at all. Frustrated, he turned to us for answers. Confused, we outsourced the problem to a consultant we heard about in India who knows a lot about sex. He also was confused, but charged us very little for his services.

What was the deal? Turns out that Johnny F. was suffering from an extreme case of anoxgasmi, or the inability to experience an orgasm in front of a paying crowd. This is a common problem, right up there with being unable to slow-dance with the elderly at bar mitzvahs, but unlike the latter, this is a dilemma that can actually be remedied without closing your eyes and holding your breath.

What to do? Simple . . .

1. Practice makes perfect. Try to have sex at as many picnics and fairs as you can, including 4-H and other child-friendly gatherings where butter-sculpting contests take place.

2. Do you have a close family friend or neighbor who might be willing to watch you have sex with a partner and then notify you with a prearranged bird call whenever you're doing something wrong? There has to be at least one, right? Maybe a schoolteacher or an artsy type?

3. Pretend that everyone in the audience is also nude and doing it doggy style while "This Is How We Do It" blasts from tiny iPod speakers. You will be amazed at how quickly things can go from excruciatingly hellish to perfectly run-of-the-mill.

Our famous canned-
fruit ambrosia! Looks
good? It *is!*

4. Know thy room! This is important. Before your sexual act, walk around the performing area and get your bearings. How will your audience see you on the stage? Will their sight lines be adequate? Or will they be blocked by the pyrotechnic explosives you rented for the afternoon? Also, please confirm that the sixteen D batteries in your multiple-speed dildo are still fresh from the previous evening's rehearsal dinner at the hotel's bar.

5. Attitude determines altitude. With a smile on your face and a gleam in your eye, you can accomplish practically anything. See that group of sad-looking adults standing on tiptoe outside the Titillation Tent? What they wouldn't give to be in your shoes, totally naked except for your sneakers, having sex in front of a paying crowd! Appreciate what you have!

6. Close your eyes and pretend that you're in that most "perfect spot," the most beautiful resort you've ever visited or have ever dreamed of visiting. In our case, this would be the company-owned one-bedroom time share in Tampa.

That's it! See ya at the picnic! (And please keep in mind that we can <u>always</u> use more non-recyclable plastic utensils!)

THINGS COMMONLY YELLED DURING ORGASM PHASE

Men

"Ta-*da*!"

"This isn't as fun as Ludacris made it sound!"

"Take that!"

"Who's the loser now, Mom?"

"This feels like a carnival ride . . . that just jumped the tracks!"

"I'll pay for that, no problemo!"

"Don't be mad, 'kay?"

"And don't come back, ya hear?"

"Now I know how Liberace must have felt!"

"No, thank *you*. The pleasure was all mine."

Women

We're not really sure. Something like jazz scatting, maybe?

HEY, DIDJA KNOW...

At the height of orgasm the brain can produce enough electricity to power a smoothie mixer?

Many card games in the 1970s involved oral sex?

In New Hampshire, a respectable blow job is a component of the driver's-license exam for both men and women?

Missionaries benefit from low expectations in bed? They'll often mix it up with side entry or something, and get all smug like they're Peter North.

An old wives' tale has proven true: If your beard turns yellow while performing cunnilingus, it means you like butter?

Clinical sexologists measure horniness on the Lupine Scale of Tongue and Eye Protuberance?

Nothing doin'.

Hello, miss!

Hot-cha!

Va-va-va-voom, it's off to da room!

CHAPTER 4

SEXUAL INTERCOURSE

EVERYTHING UP TO THE PART WHERE YOU'RE ON OPPOSITE SIDES OF THE BED, SOBBING

You've fulfilled your unspoken and contractual obligation to engage in foreplay. Now as you and your partner stare at each other's open, glistening naked-ness and prepare for the beautiful act of coitus, you both wonder: *What next? Do we just run at each other from opposite sides at full speed and violently collide in the act of lovemaking?* Yes. In essence, that is it. (Please consult our previous self-published book, *Advanced Sexual Positions, as Developed by Leading Military Experts in the Fields of Extraction and Rendition*, Poolesville Press, 2006.)

THAT FIRST TIME:
A NIGHT, AFTERNOON, OR CAR WASH TO REMEMBER

The memories that last, the ones that stay with us even when we're elderly and not sure if the fork we're holding is real or something in our dead cat's dream, often involve significant firsts. A lot becomes fuzzy over the years, but nobody who's old enough will ever forget where they were when they saw Neil Armstrong walk on the moon or what exactly they were doing when President George W. Bush wasn't shot. Why? Because that first time *changes* you.

Even if your first time was not among the tens of thousands recorded each year by ABS drone planes, it's safe to say that if you're reading this you're probably no longer a virgin. However, a few of you are holding out for that perfect soul mate or just someone who's able to endure three or four thrusts' worth of whatever it is you secrete from your pores when nervous. Or maybe you're just a bit confused, and, as we've all learned, it can be frustrating receiving five different answers to your highly personal virginity questions at five different post-office windows. So let's start at the beginning.

What *is* virginity, and what does it mean to lose it? The answer might seem obvious, yet 3 percent of people who think they're losing their virginity are actually knitting or getting a haircut. So, for the record: Conventionally speaking, to lose one's virginity is to engage in sexual intercourse for the first time. In cultures where a woman's virginity is considered a prize, the presence or absence of a membrane over the opening of the vagina is often used as an indicator. It can be misleading, as this thin lining (the hymen) can be perforated by such everyday activities as riding a bicycle or masturbating with a decorative candlestick. The virgin penis, of course, is easy to identify by the hard outer casing that encloses it like an oyster shell and that eventually dissolves. (To see this process up close, please buy or rent the 1964 nudist film *But Charlie, I Don't Play Volleyball*.)

Now that you understand the mechanics, let's talk about getting that initial sex act right. To begin with, please realize that your first partner probably won't be the person you'll eventually marry. Rather, he or she might "attend" college in a faraway state or only sleep with you as a test of willpower akin to not pulling one's hand away from an open flame. Also, be sure that the setting is conducive to lovemaking. No matter whom you're with, you'll *never* have fond memories of the event if you're getting frisky somewhere PETA was gathering clandestine video footage just two hours earlier.

The inexperienced often don't understand what intercourse is. This confused young man believes he's experiencing it right now.

Something to consider: You won't always know when the magical moment is upon you, so it's a good idea to carry a blanket, a pillow, sheets, and a box of smelling salts (optional). These items can turn any ten-meter diving platform into an on-the-go honeymoon suite. And be sure the location is at least reasonably private. Look around before you begin. Is there a good chance you'll be interrupted by passers-by on the beach or by the other Stonehenge tourists? Are there any stowaways on the catamaran you just made off with?

There's more to the first experience, of course. Have you thought about the musical choices? Mood music is *extremely* important and can be very, very helpful, especially when the music is coming from the stereo and not from blowing trumpet noises into your tightly clenched fist.

Consider the following listening selections above all others:

SONGS TO POP YOUR CHERRY TO

"This Jesus Must Die," Jesus Christ Superstar soundtrack

A Pink Floyd song with sound effects of a World War II plane bursting into flames

Audiobook of Stephen King's The Tommyknockers

"My Mummy's Dead," John Lennon

"Catchin' Beavers by the Misty Bayou," Lynyrd Skynyrd

Terry Gross on NPR (gotta be played loud!)

Kaddish, the Jewish prayer for the deceased

The opera Mozart wrote about the cuckoo bird

The opera Beethoven wrote about his border collie

"I Felt Like Smashing My Face in a Clear Glass Window," Yoko Ono

"Theme to Roots," *Doc Severinsen*

"Where Is My Home?" Czech Republic national anthem

Anything by Mandy Patinkin (recommended: "Brother, Can You Spare a Dime?")

"How'd You Like to Marry a Man with No Feet?" traditional, banjo

EASY PIANO SONGS FOR SEX

The following excerpts are from *Easy Piano Songs for Sex: Tunes in the Key of F♭ck,* the first in a series of upcoming ABS instructional manuals for those music students seeking challenging yet erotically charged melodies to play while making love. These original songs highlight right-hand finger placement, elementary key signatures, most documented fetishes, and foot-pedal positioning.

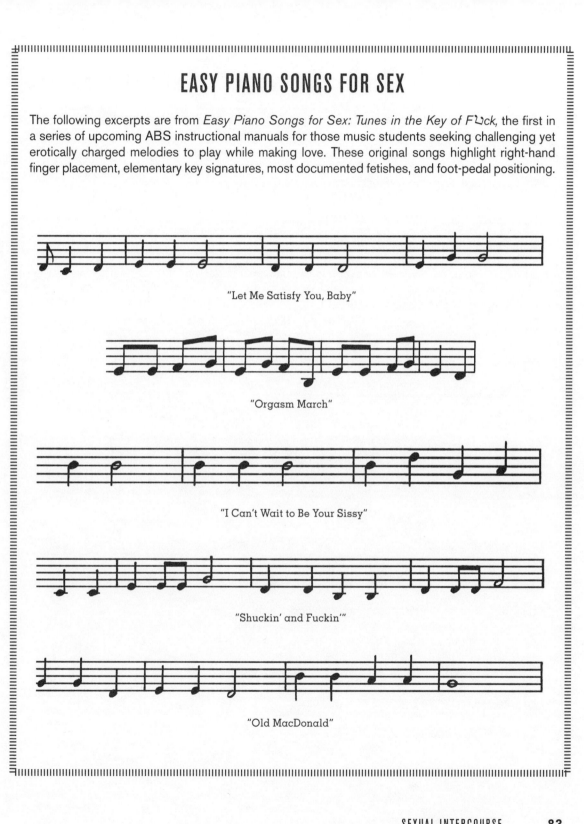

"Let Me Satisfy You, Baby"

"Orgasm March"

"I Can't Wait to Be Your Sissy"

"Shuckin' and Fuckin'"

"Old MacDonald"

DID I JUST LOSE MY VIRGINITY? A CHECKLIST

Losing your virginity can be a subtle sensation. Often, the big moment can pass without your knowledge, and pretty soon some goons are dragging you from the haunted hayride and you're thinking, *Oh, I get it. This is usually what happens after lovemaking.*

Use this checklist as a guide. If you find yourself exhibiting ten or more of the symptoms indicated below, congratulations! You've technically lost your virginity!

Symptoms of Recently-Lost Virginity:

☐ Swollen tongue

☐ Pants around ankles/Dress over head/Adult diaper in tatters

☐ Covered in stage blood and glitter

☐ Hymen missing

☐ Wallet missing

☐ Foreskin noticeably creased

☐ Knuckles chapped and bruised from fist-bumping yourself

☐ Smells like someone's been cooking *ropa vieja*

☐ Strong but fleeting sensation that you've got it "made in the shade"

☐ Insatiable craving for goat tacos

☐ New, spider-like abilities

☐ Your shift manager at Cinnabon angrily kicking at the locked employee restroom door

☐ Suddenly no longer feeling anger toward absentee father

☐ Peter Frampton's guitar pick stuck to your ass

☐ Thick nest of animal fur trapped between your teeth

☐ Yoga mat all funky

☐ Faint, distant sound of God crying

"THIS ABANDONED REFRIGERATOR SEEMS COMFY ENOUGH": THE BEST AND WORST PLACES TO LOSE IT, AS RECOMMENDED BY ABS

There is a character in the original Broadway production of *Hair* named Rattatoni, first name James. Rattatoni is a fascinating young man. Twenty-one, just arrived in New York from Nebraska and off to the Army in a few days, he befriends a ragtag group of scrounge-abouts living in the Central Park woods, who spend their days begging for scraps of hot dogs and their nights singing songs about masturbation, all the while swinging one-handed from the city's giant sycamore maples.

Enter Rhonda, a beautiful, hairless Amish midget who has dropped out of society because she didn't dig "fitting in." One night, Rhonda—drunk off razzleberry wine—forcefully takes James by his virgin wrist, brusquely leads him onto the park's carousel and spins him into a new, beautiful reality, a world where anything and everything is possible, even losing one's virginity before a group of anxious-looking children visiting from the Far East.

Rattatoni was *extremely* lucky. Magic dust was sprinkled on his first cognizant sexual experience, and he will never, ever forget it, at least until the day he's shipped off to Vietnam and then beaten to death for growing out his pubic hair in order to make a statement about the war.

How about *you*? Do you remember your first time? How did it happen, and why? Where did it happen? More importantly, did you later sing and dance about this event on a stage while enthusiastically encouraging the audience to get up out of their seats and celebrate along with you and your confused lover?

There are good places and there are bad places. There are better places and then there are *perfect* places. Assuming you haven't already lost your virginity—and, if you're younger than twenty-five, we really hope you haven't—here is a list of ABS-sanctioned locations, good, bad, and beyond.

BAD PLACES

- Luggage rack on a Greyhound bus, on the way to Lord knows where
- A stranger's bat mitzvah, smack dab in the middle of the hora circle
- Roughly six exits after stopping to pick up that drifter with the colorful past

GOOD PLACES

- On the couch at your former fraternity, homecoming weekend
- The *Jersey Boys* tour bus
- Thanksgiving at a restaurant with "All You Can Eat" in its name
- At a gang-bang-video shoot, in front of the catered "bagel nook"
- Drum circle, the finger cymbalists keeping you in perfect 4/4 time

GREAT PLACES

- Onstage at an acting workshop, having just grabbed the improv baton
- In a sweaty post-concert huddle with Blues Traveler
- In the basement of the Los Angeles Scientology Center, just beneath a huge oil painting of L. Ron sucking off Xenu

OUR CLIENTS TALK ABOUT "LOSIN' IT" (NOT THE MOVIE)

Deborah, age 38

Like every girl in my high-school class, I had a huge, huge, huge crush on the rock star Eddie Money. I would watch his video for "Take Me Home Tonight" and get so jealous of Ronnie Spector! How dare she dance so close to my Eddie? Ha ha! Well, turns out Eddie was playing a gig at the rock club downtown. I thought, This is it. I'm going backstage, and I'm going to give Eddie Money the greatest gift a young woman can give. I showed up early that night with all sorts of sneaky plans for getting back to Eddie, but to my surprise, there was no one even guarding the stage door! I walked right into Eddie's dressing room and told him how I felt. Not only did he agree to take my virginity, but he actually canceled the show and cleared his schedule for the rest of the weekend. He made love to me hungrily, like he hadn't been with a woman in months, maybe years. Afterward he begged me not to go, and he even tried to improvise a song about me on guitar. It sounded okay. The next day at school I couldn't keep my secret—I bragged to all the girls that I had actually made love to Eddie! Our Eddie! They got real quiet, and then told me that their appreciation of Eddie Money had only been ironic. Funny the things kids do.

Louise, age 70

I lost it to a greaser. We all did back in the fifties. What more is there to say? I lost it to a greaser. End of story.

Brent, age 29

Back in school I was working as a pizza-delivery boy for the Mellow Mushroom, and brother, it is true what they say! One night I delivered a pepperoni pie to this rich-person neighborhood, and who should answer the door but some smoking hot chick, and she's standing there practically naked! She says she doesn't have any cash, but how would I like to be paid in sex, straight up, down and dirty, right then and there? Cha-ching!

Lucy, age 32

As a little girl I discovered my father's pornography collection, and it warped my thinking. From what I understood, sex was what happens between a pizza boy and a woman who has no money for pizza. When I decided it was time to lose my virginity I ordered a large pepperoni pie from the Mellow Mushroom and waited. The pizza boy was hideous. Paunchy, drooling, just a loser. Kept asking how much it costs to live in a "rich-person neighborhood." Like, during the act. It was downhill from there. For a while I prostituted myself on the streets of Chicago for one and a half deep-dish pizzas a night. The remaining half-pizza went to my pimp, Ronnie.

ANYTHING WORTH DOING IS WORTH DOING LIKE A METHAMPHETAMINE-CRAZED PORN STAR:
IMPROVING YOUR SEXUAL TECHNIQUE

So you've lost your virginity. It was a pretty big deal, and we at ABS commend you (the Mylar balloon you awoke to find tied to your pinkie finger was from us). But the first time can't last forever, so to keep things interesting you have to get creative.

MASTERING THE POSITIONS

BASIC

As anyone who has had sex (or is having sex right now) will tell you, there are really only three basic sexual positions:

DOMINANT

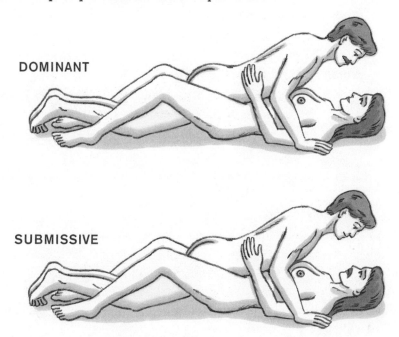

SUBMISSIVE

JUST GIVING UP
(a recently discovered sexual position that provides equal effort from—and pleasure to—both partners)

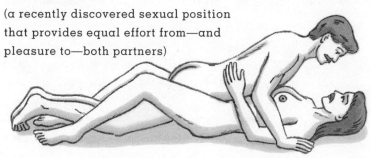

Try these three basic positions repeatedly, in a variety of combinations, until you feel confident enough to move on to the following, more complex coital configurations.

INTERMEDIATE

Jester Entering Palace

Slight variation on the missionary position. Here, the dominant partner uses humor to disarm his lover, then slyly enters her. After prematurely ejaculating, the Dominant Partner makes a quick, self-effacing joke, and then "exits the palace with great haste," all the while coughing nervously.

Worshipping the Idol

The male lies supine as his lover straddles him. The male grasps her hips firmly, not unlike a peasant clutching at an idol. As his lover begins to rock back and forth, the male prematurely ejaculates. Only when the penis has lost all rigidity does the female dismount, a goddess made flesh by eleven seconds or so of quasi-ecstasy.

Knife and Spoon

The male and female lie on their sides, facing the same direction. The female parts her legs slightly, affording her lover entrance from the rear. Presenting herself in this manner proves highly erotic, and the male prematurely ejaculates before penetrating. Carefully and quietly, the male spoons the ejaculate into his palm and then attempts to nonchalantly drizzle it along his lover's back.

The Jade Butterfly and the Prematurely Ejaculating Serpent

The dominant partner faces his lover and, upon entering her, fully arches his back to prolong copulation by avoiding the unfortunate intimacy of eye contact. When this fails, the dominant partner prematurely ejaculates—in this position, this is called "molting"—and then collapses upon his bemused lover in a stinky, sweaty heap, all the while applauding a job well done.

BLACK DIAMOND

The following sexual positions, while all equally capable of unlocking phantasmagoric pleasures, are considered highly dangerous and should be attempted only under controlled circumstances, such as on national TV or in the presence of one of this book's authors:

Three Figs in a Basket

Multitasking While Filling Out a Sudoku Puzzle

The Cure for Feline Leukemia

There Will Be Blood

The Kennedy Center Honors

Searching for the Missing Loot

Sin Is Such a Sneaky Little Character

Another Lame Twist in an M. Night Shyamalan Movie

I Need to Wear These Driving Gloves Because of My Eczema

What Uncle Carl Taught Me the Summer I Was Supposed to Be Working at His Lawn-Care Company

Hurry, I'm Due Back at the Piercing Pagoda

Capturin' Critters with a Big Stick

Applying for Much-Needed Government Aid

Saving that Last Chocolate Cupcake for the Babysitter

Warning: Discontinue the practice of any of the previous positions if either you or your partner experience one of the following symptoms:

- Light-headedness
- Shortness of breath
- Blood in stool
- Loose change in stool
- Seeing yourself on a viral video
- Offering strangers "free hugs"
- Tears in your anus at ten and two o'clock
- Hallucinations that involve the cast of *The Golden Girls*
- Uncontrollable ejaculation
- Uncontrollable somersaults
- Gigantism
- Sweaty elbows
- Growth of rigid, spiny plates around your belly button
- Existential ennui
- A sense of olfactory certainty that someone, somewhere nearby, is cooking a turkey loaf

THE CALMER SUTRA: SAFE AND SANE POSITIONS FOR *NORMAL* PEOPLE

There's nothing wrong with a little experimentation now and then—as long as it's kept well within the bounds of normalcy. But that most venerable of sex manuals, the *Kama Sutra*, is just so exotic. It's all *lotus* this and *yoni* that, and what kind of language is *yoni*, anyway? Puerto Rican?

Forget prehistoric history. Your sex life exists in the here and now, in a neighborhood with good schools and with easy access to a coffee shop in which to write your romance novel. If you know how to look for it, all the sexual variation you need is already right there in your everyday routine. Take these examples:

Gated Community

The man pantomimes the presentation of proper ID to his partner, who, lying on her side, slowly raises her top leg like the bar at a security checkpoint. Authorized insertion may now take place.

Congress of a Riding Lawn Mower

With the female on all fours, the male squats behind her and penetrates from behind, occasionally withdrawing to check on a weird grinding noise that's probably the blade hitting a rock or something.

Twining of a Curly Fry

In this gentle position, the woman coils her arms and legs around her lover, one greasy curly fry entangled with another, now indivisible in love.

It is so easy to make your own positions! Just ask yourself questions like, "What would it be like to make love while holding a walking stick? Or, with a cinnamon toothpick still dangling from the lower lip? Or, after 9:30 p.m.?" Work with your partner and let your imagination run wild—and leave all that missionary stuff to the good people bringing the light of Christ to primitives, okay?

INTERNATIONAL COURSE

We here at ABS are often asked about sexual practices in different countries, which we find some-what odd, since we have only been outside the United States twice: once to Epcot, and another time to the European-themed Busch Gardens for Secretaries' Day. (No, secretaries were not al-lowed to attend. We have to explain this every damn year!)

The two most common questions we receive are "How do Syrian chicks like it?" (it varies) and "Is it true that you can give a prostate massage to the conductor in lieu of monetary subway fare throughout Malaysia?" (it's strongly encouraged). But hands down, what people want to know third most often is how American sex stacks up against the rest of the world. That's a complex question, and, like most complicated questions, there is no way to successfully answer it.

This chart, however, should offer—at the very least—some insight into foreign sex practices.

COUNTRY	SEXUAL PROCLIVITY
Serbia	A black leather cap will identify you as a "leather queen," but if paired with leather pants, people may mistake you for someone who special-izes in emergency dentistry.
Somalia	There is a "hanky code," but it doesn't involve rear-pocket placement. Instead, it is tied around the neck of your lead goat, which can be rented by the hour.
China	Laughing in public means you want a blow job. Crying in public means you've just given one.
Jamaica	Public-restroom "foot-tap code" is performed with a tiny steel drum.
Iceland	Sex in public is permitted if you keep a live cat safely inside your cashmere sweater at all times.
Japan	Drinking cow's milk in Japan will make you appear to have the counte-nance of a chubby woman who frowns upon promiscuity.
Turkey	If you wish to receive anal sex, just wear a beret and hum Journey's classic "Stone in Love."
Netherlands	Do not, under any circumstances, stick your thumb inside a lesbian in the Netherlands.
Thailand	Asking for a "Snickers" will get you two hours in a "sex coffin" with an elderly custodian, which is considered extremely good luck.
Canada	Walking around with three fingers in your mouth is "cruising code" for being on the prowl, but walking around with only two fingers in your mouth means you're simple.

PELVIC EXERCISES TO HELP HIM PUMP FASTER

Sexually experienced men and women agree: the key to incredible sex is a good sixty to seventy minutes of powerful, rapid-fire, hell-bent-for-leather pumping (often accompanied by a glassy stare and labored, put-upon sighs). If you're a woman whose lover pumps too softly, or just a man interested in upping your PPS (pumps per second) rate, you may want to try these fun and easy couples' exercises.

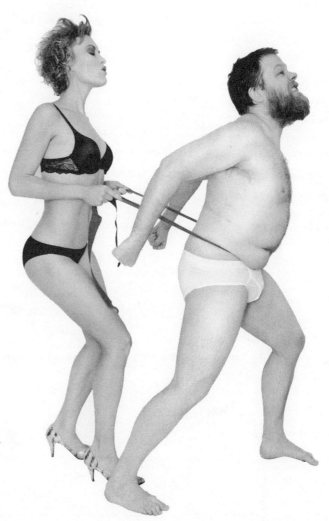

BREAKING THE TAPE
The man stands in place, and, using only the movement of his hips, pretends he is a marathon runner repeatedly crossing the finish line. For extra authenticity, try making love afterward while sweating buckets under a space blanket.

BEANIE BUDDY

While she provides dynamic
resistance in a beanbag chair,
he crouches low and, with quick,
staccato thrusts, nudges her across
a smooth surface. Twenty or thirty
yards should do the trick.

WATCH YOUR DRINKS

(For advanced thrusters only)
With one smooth, strong
backward pump, he yanks
the tablecloth off her dinner
table, while miraculously
leaving all plates, wine
goblets, candelabras, and,
yes, onion loaves standing.

HOW DEEPLY ARE YOU PENETRATING?

IS IT ENOUGH?

It pains us here at ABS to think that millions of men around the world still use their penises just as they might use an automobile's oil dipstick: pulling it out, wiping the thing halfheartedly against a cheap paper towel, dropping the towel, squirting a dab of antiseptic lotion onto their hands, nodding at another gentleman standing a few yards away, writing down the results in a small notebook, flicking on a classic rock station midway through a Jefferson Airplane deep cut, and then getting on with their damn business.

When it comes to sexual intercourse—or anything, really—just how well a man plunges his penis into a vagina is *very* important. If you don't believe us, you might want to hold an informal phone poll, just as we did the night before writing this book. Here's what we found: 60 percent of the women we called said that it was "very important" for a man to plunge properly, 20 percent of the women felt that it was "somewhat important," and the rest of the high-school seniors took down our names and Twitter accounts, and promised to get "connected" later.

Now (before we get even more technical) here is a truncated history on genitals, building on what we've already covered in Chapter 1.

Penises and vaginas have had a very long and complicated relationship over the past few thousand years. You can think of them as comically mismatched roommates. The penis is the messy one, the one who prefers things just as they are, disorganized though they may be; the vagina is the prissy little missy who becomes furious when the apartment is left untidy after a long night of poker.

As a rule, the penis is *always* content. The vagina, however, is moody, and prone to outbursts and xenophobic attacks against outside agitators. With this in mind, the sex act has to be a perfect storm of thrust, direction, degree, and pitch. Also yaw and roll. One false move and you're going to end up eating the donut by the gilly wagon. We're not sure what this expression means, but the carnival worker we overheard saying it seemed sexually savvy enough.

You could do a hell of a lot worse than talking to this guy about the vagina.

Getting to the crux of this section, if you're a man and you're having sex with a woman, how can you go about making a vagina happy? How deeply should the penis be thrust, and how can you tell if your penis is doing its difficult, messy job down there in that bizarro world invisible to all of us but that most mystical of sexual seers, Rabbi Shmuley Boteach of Englewood, New Jersey?

Answer: You can't. Simply jab away like a famished chimpanzee poking a twig into an anthill, and pray for the best.

AFTER IT'S ALL OVER:

NOW *WHAT? SMALL TALK AND THE SEARCH FOR THE OVERHEAD-FAN REMOTE*

Your pulse is slowing. Your eyes are bulging less and are approximately half as insane-looking. The frilly Dutch milkmaid hat your lover is wearing—though it sent blood surging into your genitals just a few short moments ago—suddenly strikes you as a tad ridiculous. In short, you've just performed the sex act. What next?

As usual, that depends. Many couples proceed from intercourse directly into a private sex debriefing. These debriefings can be carried out anywhere, but typically are held close to where the actual sex occurred, often while seated in office-style chairs on opposite sides of a a table (couples may want to set their debriefing table in advance with Altoids, fresh pitchers of ice water, and, should the situation call for them, embossed name cards). The debriefing is the time to address questions such as the following:

- "Which of your guttural blurted statements should I be most concerned about?"
- "Is this going to be a thing tomorrow morning back on the killing floor?"
- "Why do you keep referring to them as my 'crap flaps'?"
- "Do you think the pets noticed what we were doing? I only ask because the dogs are still baying and nervously thumping their tails on the floor."

Some couples think sex debriefings are too impersonal, and prefer a post-coital song or poem. Light verse or epic poetry, cute-as-the-dickens nursery rhyme or funky ad-libbed jive chatter— the style doesn't matter, only the sentiment. For example, after a recent lovemaking session, one of the authors sat nude before his lover and recited the following:

You, my lover
Me, my lover's love!
Your hair, damp with salty lovesweat
Your maiden fur, tousled sweetly by mine own fingers
O lover!
O lover's cries!
Shall we again, my lover, revert to the altar where I keep my
stanky potions?

Notice what he did here: the repetition of the word "lover" for maximum tenderness; the use of the arcane but highly erotic term "maiden fur" rather than the mood-killing "big ol' bush"; lots of exclamation points. Simply put, this is hot stuff. Especially if recited while beating slowly on a bass drum with a slender rubber dildo.

Dreams . . . A Great Place to Have Sex

Accredited in over
thirty townships

By Michael Kupperman, Clinical Psychologist

As a psychologist, I hear all types of sex dreams. Many of my patients like to start their sessions with one, and I try to be receptive. "What's the latest sex dream?," I'll ask, and then I'll feign enthusiasm as they ramble on and on. But many of these stories feature poor story logic, and are unappealing in their texture or emotional syntax. There's no wow factor. Still, I have to be polite.

For hundreds of years people didn't dream about sex; they dreamed about bears and fish. Then along came a fellow named Sigmund Freud. He pointed out that a lot of these bears and fish were behaving in sexually provocative ways. In Freud's view the human head is like a house, with an unfinished attic called the subconscious, where tiny people called "subconscii" live. They come down out of the attic when we're asleep, Freud claimed, and they mess around, enacting weird little scenarios that are really about sex in disguise. Freud became the daddy of sex-dream theorization, and I'll bet he made a bundle.

"The pickle sandwich that's winking at you in your dreams, that represents something," claimed Freud. Everything represented something sexual. If you dreamed about sex with a moth, that meant you wanted to have sex with your mother while a moth watched. Freud believed that anything in dreams that was in the form of a container, such as an antique whatnot chest filled with your grandmother's remains, could hold a penis, and maybe even several, if you arranged the cremation ashes just so.

Later, or possibly at the same time, another man named Carl Jung had some additional theories. To him dreams represented "Archie Types." In other words, all of us dream of being either Archie, Reggie, Jughead, Betty, Veronica, Big Ethel, Moose, Principal Weatherbee, or Richard "Poppy" Svenson, the janitor. Sexual dreams represent our desires to have sex with other comic-book characters, he believed. That guy made a mint.

Today's dream landscape is littered with foreign material, some accidental, some not. We're all used to having the occasional sex dream about a taxi dispatcher or a handicapped tree surgeon. But every night thousands, if not millions, of people dream that 1980s-era Tony Danza is out on a date with an orangutan who can flip the bird and do funny cartwheels.

In reality, this is a test transmission that NASA made in 1985 that got bounced off the moon and ended up trapped in toilet tanks. If you sleep less than twelve feet from a toilet tank, you're gonna experience this in your lifetime. This is distinct from deliberate transmissions perpetrated by spoiled Hollywood actors. Many celebrities have satellites in orbit, beaming sexually suggestive scenarios featuring themselves directly into thousands of sleeping heads. If you dream of sex with a famous person, let them know you don't appreciate it. Find out where they live, and go there with your lawyer. A smart celebrity will pay big to have their dream intrusion go unreported. Jeff Foxworthy once paid me a million dollars to keep quiet about a dream concerning a shoe that was also a vagina. And a swamp eel. I signed a confidentiality agreement that I would never, ever mention that specific dream in print.

Oh well.

SEX WITHOUT THE EMPHYSEMA: POST-COITAL ALTERNATIVES TO SMOKING

Sex is one of the most beautiful and healthy activities you can do without taking off your business attire. In fact, when it comes to calories burned, sex-as-exercise ranks just behind ping-pong (225 calories per week), Chinese checkers (156 calories over a lifetime), and absentmindedly swiping some crumbs off your lap (zero). So why ruin such a good thing with a post-coital ciggy? There are alternatives, all of which are listed here. (There are no others, so please don't bother.)

- Performing push-ups while chanting a particularly ribald infantry cadence. (Try personalizing it for your partner, i.e., "I don't know but I've been told, my husband's member is fun to hold! Hooya!")

- Creating Smipples, a series of hobbit-like creatures created by dipping each others' nipples in finger paints and pressing firmly against construction paper. Suggested Smipple names: Zach, Wingy, Puddles.

- Checking the windows for peepers.

- If peepers are found, teaching them a sexy lesson using a Japanese paper fan as a paddle.

- Enjoying a bowl of vegetarian baked beans.

- Taking off your orange wristband that reads FLIGHT RISK.

SEX AND YOUR DAILY CONCERNS:
LET ABS HELP

SEX-PROOFING YOUR HOME

Perhaps the greatest joy of buying a home is being in possession of so many thrilling new places to have intercourse: sinks, sconces, jam cellars, atop the utility shelving the previous owner left in the carport, the toilets. *Ahhhh . . .* the toilets!

An imaginative couple can put the dankest crawl space to use for a grubby game of "earthworm's delight," or turn a boring, soot-smeared chimney into a tall, breezy fuck perch. But be careful! Even before the first scrotal imprint is left on the medicine cabinet, the following precautions should be taken to sex-proof your new home.

KITCHEN

- Zesters, whisks, and strawberry hullers make fine impromptu sex toys. Cheese graters, bagel cutters, and meat tenderizers do not. (Carrot peelers, of course, can go either way, and often do.)
- Never place your lover's bare backside on a chopping board where jalapeños have just been seeded and chopped.
- Most important, when doing it on top of the stove, make sure to turn the handles of all boiling pots *away* from the sex. Also, consider checking whatever dish you happen to be cooking at the time. Think about it: That bubbling pot of gumbo ain't gonna wait until *after* you climax, *mon cher.*

LIVING ROOM/FAMILY ROOM

- Cover all electrical outlets, especially if your sex play involves thrusting metal rods wildly in all directions.
- Cover the controls for the TV and stereo. There's nothing worse than accidentally mashing a button and having your plunging spoiled by a snippet of C-SPAN's *Booknotes*.
- Avoid any hard, stand-up pounding against load-bearing walls or Ikea products.

BATHROOM

- Place non-slip safety mats not only in the shower but in any area you plan on making wet.
- Might as well brush and gargle real quick.
- When a sex toy falls behind the toilet, observe the three-second rule. (When a sex toy falls *in* the toilet, observe the one-second rule.)

BEDROOM

- Sex in a bedroom is considered pedestrian and not advised, unless other rooms have been rendered uninhabitable (for example, if your kitchen is being sprayed for earwigs, or a group of traveling magazine salesmen has permanently moved into your living room).

BEYOND THE DOORKNOB SOCK:
SEX SIGNIFIERS FOR THE SOPHISTICATE

Communication between partners is the key to great sex, but as we've already mentioned it's every bit as important to communicate about your sex life with the people *around* you: your landlady, your randomly assigned roommate at the men's hotel, the neighborhood teenager paid to hose down that old rabbit hutch and haul it to the dump, etc. If the message you mean to get across is as simple as "I am currently having sex mere feet away from you," you can rely on the old college-dormitory trick of hanging a necktie or sock on the doorknob. Alternatively, you can go with a more nuanced signal.

Translation: "I'm having sex in here, and I drank all the milk. Be a dove and pick up another quart?"

Translation: "You're going to hear someone shrieking like a colicky newborn. Don't freak! It's part of our thing."

Translation: "I'm having sex in here, but feel free to come on in and fix my laptop; it's been a little wonky."

Translation: "Here's a photo of the sex I'm having inside. How'm I doin'? ;)"

HEY, DIDJA KNOW ...

With proper lubrication and attachment, the act of intercourse can double as a makeshift rock tumbler?

The phrase "young, dumb, and full of cum" is often falsely attributed to John Keats?

More than half of penetrations occur within five miles of home?

Humanity's very last sexual penetration will occur on May 6, 3022, in the early morning hours, immediately following a Cinco de Mayo party in Arlington, Virginia?

The conjoined twins Chang and Eng had no problem having sex in front of each other, but were totally unable to tinkle without launching into a fit of the giggles?

CHAPTER 5

MASTURBATION

SEXUALITY'S
MIDGET SIDEKICK

Throughout history, masturbation—known as "Dutch sex" in the pornographic and medical fields—has had its ups and downs in terms of public acceptance.

Many early civilizations thought of masturbation as natural, and even beneficial for enhancing one's sexual potency. (Most, if not all, of these civilizations are now gone.) A pictograph discovered in Thailand's Nakhon Sawan province, dating back to the fifth millennium B.C., depicts a young male masturbating in a bathing hut while his mother stands outside the locked thatch door, demanding to know how it could possibly take this long for her son to detangle his hair.

Ancient Egyptians gave male masturbation (or, as they referred to it, "mummifying the cat god") a spiritual significance, believing that the mythological deity Atum created the universe from his own ejaculate. To honor this god, Egyptian pharaohs were required to ceremonially masturbate into the Nile, which was convenient for those pharaohs who were already masturbating into the Nile for recreational purposes. Some claim this is why beaches along the Nile were extremely unpopular and still, to this day, smell faintly of bleach.*

In the West, attitudes toward masturbation remained liberal through the sixteenth century—for instance, it was not uncommon for audiences at Shakespeare's Globe Theatre to praise an actor's performance by ejaculating during a soliloquy. It is said that during an early performance of the death scene from *Romeo and Juliet*, an awed hush fell over the theater, leaving only the rustling taffeta and gentle clacking of Queen Elizabeth I rubbing one out in the gallery.

By 1760, public opinion took a negative turn, thanks to the publication of *L'Onanisme*, a medical treatise on the ill effects of masturbation, written by Samuel Tissot. (Tissot also holds the distinction of being Europe's most face-punched gentleman.) The study linked

*Personal observation.

masturbation to a variety of maladies, including impaired vision, gout, that weird tickle in your ear like before you get a cold, and advanced Semitism.

Today we know that masturbation (like Semitism) never was, and never will be, an indication of a lousy sex life. Think of it as a *complement* to your sex life, rather than as a stand-in. If sex is an exquisitely prepared seven-course meal—and the orgasm a satisfying after-dinner bowel movement—then masturbation is a Swanson Salisbury-steak TV dinner for one . . . no less delectable than intercourse, but often better enjoyed alone on a stained futon, in grim silence.

A popular eighteenth-century anti-masturbation device.

This chapter will cover prevailing attitudes about masturbation, as well as tips and techniques to enhance your (and, in the case of mutual masturbation, your partner's) enjoyment. As the Dutch might say, *"Laten gaan van mijn warme hond!"*

Now, after carefully digesting the important material in this chapter, and after translating the above phrase, go forth and masturbate!

DEBUNKING MASTURBATION MYTHS

While ABS's educational outreach has gone a long way toward puncturing the falsehoods surrounding masturbation, the fact remains that bad information has been circulating for so long, and to such a degree, that it's now become embedded in our common understanding of self-love. So, for the credulous among you, let's clear a few things up once and for all.

If you masturbate, you'll go blind.

This is just patently false. For the last time, there is no connection between masturbation and blindness, period. Do not blame your blindness on masturbation or vice versa. Though, to be safe, never masturbate more than a few steps away from an emergency eyewash station.

If you masturbate, you'll get hair on your palms.

Unless you're incorporating a gorilla puppet into the act (highly recommended), there is no chance of this happening.

If you masturbate, you'll get acne all over your body.

Really? We hadn't heard this one. Seems totally bogus, of course, but kinda makes you think twice, doesn't it?

If you masturbate, you'll become impotent.

You're joking, right? For real? Impotent? We haven't noticed this, but maybe it just hasn't happened yet. Is it reversible? Is it like smoking, where if you stop early enough, you can undo all the damage? Well, go ask that guy who told you! Fuck.

Every time you masturbate, a kitten dies.

Why, God, why? Why does it have to be this way?!!!

"NO, OFFICER— I WAS MERELY CHECKING FOR TICKS":
HOW TO MASTURBATE PUBLICLY AND AVOID DETECTION

The urge to masturbate can strike at any time, anywhere, and we are helpless to control it. But what if that itch presents itself, say, on a trolley car or in front of a tantalizing SnackWell's display at your local grocery store? Should you resist and deny yourself a basic human pleasure simply because masturbating in public is considered taboo and a good reason to get hauled out of the inflatable moon bounce? Not necessarily.

Just be smart. Adhering to certain sensible and practical precautions when self-pleasuring in a public space can mean the difference between experiencing the heights of ecstasy or feeling the kiss of a constable's truncheon upon your wrists (which, admittedly, can still be deliciously, erotically charged).

Consider these tricks of the trade:

The Bully's Comeuppance

While violently masturbating in line at Sephora, misdirect public concern by presenting your pleasure as a form of punishment. Punctuate each strum or yank with a resolute "You picked the wrong fella to mess with!" As you climax, don't forget to declare loudly, "Apology *accepted,* asshole!"

It's Worse Than You Think

If you receive any sideways glances while throttling yourself toward orgasm, use this as the perfect opportunity to gain the public's sympathy. Simply announce, "It's worse than you think," and then quickly append a worst-case scenario that makes the fact that you're masturbating in a laser-tag arena seem like an act of selfless charity by comparison. For example, "This is the *only* way I know how to celebrate Hitler's birthday."

The Nightfly

Camouflage yourself by standing behind a larger person who is also masturbating at the Donald Fagen concert. That way, if anyone receives a rude look during "International Geophysical Year," it surely won't be *you.*

FIVE PUBLIC PLACES YOU CAN MASTURBATE WITHOUT EVER BEING DETECTED

1. Pet section of Walmart

2. Fixin's Bar at a Roy Rogers

3. Meet-and-greet for users of Friendster.com

4. Loretta Swit's star on the Hollywood Walk of Fame

5. Absolutely anywhere in Grand Rapids, Michigan

The High-Concept Approach

Instead of attempting to hide your act of pleasure, place it front and center by telling everyone else on the Pirates of the Caribbean ride that an urban terrorist has just attached an explosive device to your genitals that, unfortunately, will detonate unless you furiously disarm it. State this convincingly, and your orgasm will receive a hero's welcome instead of the usual chorus of razzes and boos.

HOW MUCH MASTURBATION IS *TOO* MUCH MASTURBATION?

Overindulgence is relatively new to humans. In our earliest years, we had to be lean and alert to stay alive. Nothing made a cheetah's day more than a *Homo habilis* waddling back to his cave with a third helping of pecan pie. Now, of course, we usually don't face immediate consequences for what we do to our bodies—we realize we've eaten too much only when we've just experienced a debilitating stroke or when we are unable to leave our bedroom without a little help from the volunteer fire department. But it's difficult to say how masturbation does us any harm in the present or in the future. We manipulate our genitals for a few minutes, experience a rapturous surge of endorphins, and then resume our address to the United Nations a bit more focused. Is there any harm in that? No, and therein lies its seductive danger.

Twenty-nine-year-old Glenn says, "I never considered my masturbation a problem. When people said they did it before bed, I just assumed they meant for the nine hours prior, like I did." So how do you know if you, like hardworking Glenn, are really doing it *too* much? Don't go by the clock. A clock is fabulous for making sure that you're in front of the TV when that show about getting anally raped in an overseas prison is about to begin, but that's about it. Instead, listen to the people around you . . . the ones your habit affects most.

IF YOU REGULARLY HEAR . . .	YOU'RE PROBABLY MASTURBATING . . .
"How come you never use that nice bull-riding machine with the attached penis I got you for Hanukkah?"	NOT ENOUGH
"I can't imagine you masturbating."	JUST RIGHT
"I'm not sure an ATM transaction requires you to tickle your balls like that."	A BIT MUCH
"Every time I try to have a serious conversation with you, you hump a Tempur-Pedic pillow to completion."	TOO MUCH
"This running to the bathroom with a latex vagina/anus hybrid every twenty minutes is really beginning to affect your surgical career, doc."	TOO, TOO MUCH

LITTLE-KNOWN MASTURBATION SLANG

Jimmy-ing your Belushi

Going on tour with Midnight Oil

Taking issue with the downstairs neighbor, Dr. Pud

Not doing your part in the whole continuation-of-species thing

Revving up Papa's engine into the red zone while still in the garage

Making the most of your mini-staycation

Finally kicking Pete Best out of the group

Setting the hounds of hell free from their temporary confinement

CREATIVE GRIPS FOR THE ADVANCED ONANIST

For a chimpanzee, masturbation isn't about technique; it's about possessing a rudimentary opposable thumb and knowing how to use it. But we humans aren't satisfied with the simple pleasures of squatting on a rock with our genitals in our fist, grinning for the children and easily offended nannies at the zoo. While some people stick with the basics, simply getting from A to orgasm isn't enough for the rest of us straight arrows.

What follows are a few highly recommended masturbation moves (as first seen on our late-night cable-access show *ABS Presents: Secret Tricks with Paw Paw*).

FOR MEN

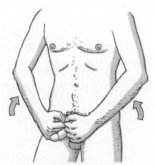

Clashing Rocks

Approach your penis from both sides with your fists. Hold it firmly in the grooves between your second and third knuckles. From there, either yank outward and away from your body as you would in a conventional masturbation stroke, or swing your arms from side to side, elbows out, as if dancing to a sea shanty.

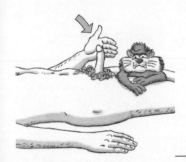

The Crane Machine

Lying on your back, allow one hand to lazily graze upon your erect penis. Nudge the miniature plush Tasmanian Devil you've carefully positioned near your testicles before realigning your fingers over the tip of your member. Close your fingers lightly, almost wispily, and wrench. Let your grip slacken, lift your hand from your penis, and repeat the process until you climax, or the Tasmanian Devil needs washing.

Scissors Beats Paper

Lay one hand flat over the penis. Spread the index and middle fingers of the other hand into a V shape (the "scissors"), and pinch both your flat hand and your penis (the "paper") within its agreeable grip. Pleasure yourself as usual. There are no losers.

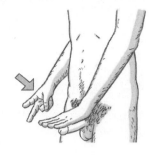

FOR WOMEN

Raiding Al Capone's Vault

Mount a tiny night-vision camera around the middle finger of your right hand. Now, with that same finger, circle the rim of the vaginal opening for twenty-five to thirty minutes, teasing the excitement of what's yet to come. Finally, insert the camera inside yourself and, with the tenacity of investigative journalist Geraldo Rivera, root around furiously as if searching for hidden cash or antique Tommy guns. Watch the live feed on a nearby portable monitor with a crowd of buddies. Wait for the climax that may or may not ever arrive.

Backup on the 101

With one hand stimulating the clitoris, use your free hand to reach into a shoebox filled with miniature Matchbox cars and trucks (no boats, please) and insert the vehicles inside you, one by one, until you've "blocked the lane." For an extra kick of ecstasy, pop a miniature replica of the General Lee from Dukes of Hazzard *into your "HOV lane" (anus) and sit back and feel that South-of-the-Mason Dixie rush.*

The Seventh Plague of Egypt

Warm your fingertips by gripping a radiator or caressing the grate of a space heater. Then, with your hands hovering just above the opening to your vagina, simulate the fiery hail that Moses summoned in the book of Exodus by drumming your heated fingertips upon your clitoris. While the drumming should reach a wrathful intensity, it should remain insufficient to persuade Pharaoh to set the Jews free.

THERE IS NO "I" IN "MUTUAL MASTURBATION":
THE BEST OF BOTH WORLDS

Often the frantic, leg-flailing, pubis-thrusting hurly-burly of two-person sex can be, well . . . a bit much. Just because you're in the mood to get your rocks off with a partner doesn't mean you're ready to commit to the physical equivalent of making life-size marionette puppets appear to swing-dance. For these laid-back occasions, mutual masturbation comes in mighty handy. *Anyone* can do it. In fact, it's one of the few sex acts to make the list of "Low-Impact Games for Sleepy Elderly" in *AARP: The Magazine* (just after "Brushing teeth to the rhythm of 'Shave and a Haircut'").

Try this with your lover: lie side by side on your backs, preferably atop a surface no less comfortable than a posture-adjustable harem bed with a generous assortment of tasseled body pillows. Now place your hands on each others' genitals and go to sleep for ten to twelve hours. Chances are that merely through normal REM spasms and the occasional violent night terror you will succeed in masturbating each other before you even awake. If this doesn't occur, you shouldn't get discouraged . . . yet it *does* mean you have some work to do.

Now, allowing your fingers to go limp and floppy like rabbits dangling from a bow hunter's gutting rack, reassert your hands' places on each other's genitals. While staring into the middle distance and imagining whatever it is you imagine during these situations (if at a loss, try thinking about nude, fully shaven postal workers with prominent musculature and unnaturally dark suntans), allow your hand to play upon your lover's pubic region—spastically, but not without some appearance of idiot joy, like a three-year-old bopping uncomprehendingly to a simpleton playing a fiddle.

Thaaaat's it. That's mutual masturbation! Now just keep doing that to each other until both of you climax, or one of you shouts, "Fine, just do it *yourself*, then! I'm off to the farmers' market! Do we still need organic honeydew?"

IT'S HIP TO 'BATE!:
ABS TALKS TO KIDS

We at ABS are passionate believers in the therapeutic power of masturbation, and we'll go even further: Not only should masturbation be taught in school, it should also be an organized extracurricular activity. Junior varsity *and* varsity. Does that blow your mind? Get over it, squares.

That's right, it's hip to 'bate! And more of today's youth need to know what they're missing. According to several articles we've read in various free publications handed out in lesbian-owned yoga centers, today's kids are *way* overstimulated. Violent video games, independent films, Mexican comic books, and ticklin' parties: Teenagers today live in a world that, metaphorically speaking, constantly strokes their penis or lays a finger upon their clitoris. Little wonder, then, that today's generation of kids doesn't make the necessary time or effort to huddle in locked rooms and furtively stimulate themselves to orgasm!

If you have a child in his or her teens, it's your responsibility to offer the 411 on masturbation. (Call it "the 411" when addressing your kids—they will respect that.) If your child resists—probably by saying something like "Wacking be wack" or "Naw, Clyde, that's out, *waaaaay* out, dig me?"—slap him or her soundly on the face. Then gently enumerate the many benefits of masturbation, from vise-like hand strength ("All the better to grip your video-game joysticks, Junior") to a richer fantasy life ("Maybe you can imagine that Van Der Beek character you've been carrying on about, right, kiddo?").

As a last resort, do what zoologists do with pandas who refuse to mate: show your kids images of people masturbating, and pray they get the idea. Oh, we're not suggesting that you directly expose your children to pornography, but there's no harm in, say, "mistakenly" leaving open a browser window that just "happens" to be set to LemmeSeeYaJerkIt.com.

In parenting, as in masturbation, sometimes a lighter touch is best.

SURVIVORS' STORIES:

DAREDEVILS AND NUMSKULLS SHARE THEIR TALES OF RISKY SOLO SEX THAT NEARLY ENDED IN DISASTER

Rick, age 32

"There were two things on my bucket list, and, just by coincidence, they were written one after the other. When I saw them on the page like that, I said, "Hoo boy, I gotta combine these, it's just too right!" Anyways, the two things were "Go over Niagara Falls in a barrel" and "Masturbate inside a barrel." So, naturally I decided to try it! Well, six months later I regained consciousness only to learn that the doctors had had to amputate everything below my navel due to the massive crushing injuries I had sustained. Gotta put this out there for the kiddies reading this: If you're really set on trying this fool stunt, at the very least do yourself the decency of using a specially constructed, reinforced barrel, and not a novelty barrel—used to store horehound candies—that you swiped from a Cracker Barrel restaurant! This is a cliché, but it bears repeating."

Cindy, age 44

"In my quest to successfully insert the largest-ever sex toy inside myself, I failed. It was a 55-inch midnight-blue dildo, "Dr. Strangelove," and it damn near killed me. I just really wanted something to tell the grandkids, but guess I'll just have to stick with the story about the time I rolled off the roof while masturbating to Orion's Belt."

Kirk, age 58

"I'm sure you're familiar with the Fleshlight? Cylindrical, flashlight-size toy with realistic vaginal opening and soft, fleshy insides? I absolutely swear by my Fleshlight, but recently I invested in a similar device: the Hermos. As the name suggests, it's roughly the size of a standard camping Thermos, with all the comfort and fuckability of the Fleshlight and the added benefit of being insulated from heat and cold. Really comes in handy for outdoor winter jacks, high-altitude spanks, the odd hot-doggin' wank on the rim of a volcano, what have you. Last week I was up at my masturbation retreat on North Dakota's frigid Lake Sakakawea, and I'm happy to report my Hermos functioned quite admirably, even within that corrugated ice-fishing shack."

Dorothy, age 53

"I have been married six times, twice to the same man, once to a young Indian boy named Ballyhoo. I am prone to laziness and will often refuse to leave my bedroom for days or even decades at a time. Alcohol makes me rammy. When angry or confused, I refer to my anus as a 'baby dragon's nest.' I have never had sexual intercourse; just the thought of it makes me physically ill, and I will curl into an extremely tight ball and slam my fists against my cheeks until the potential recipient leaves me alone to take someone else's food order. What was the question again?"

FIVE ROCK CLASSICS YOU DIDN'T REALIZE CONCERNED MASTURBATION

1. "Candle in the Wind," by Elton John. The imagery is pretty clear: John's "candle" burns out after a hot-to-trot sex romp with someone named Norma Jean. (The 1997 version swaps sexy Norma for the recently deceased Princess Diana. Poor taste, Elton.)

2. "Tears in Heaven," by Eric Clapton. Guess they don't call him "Slowhand" for nothing! Clapton goes gaga for a lady so smokin' hot she's like some kind of heavenly angel, alive only in his dreams. Weak-willed Clapton can't help but cry. (Compare with "Simply Irresistible," by the late, great Robert Palmer.)

3. "Lucy in the Sky with Diamonds," by the Beatles. The title's initials are L.S.D., which stands for "light self-dickhandling." To this day, the song remains very controversial and misunderstood.

4. "Gonna Rub 1 Out 4 U," by Prince. This is the finest of Prince's roughly 1,579 funk-rock masturbation anthems, just after "I Want U 2 Go Out 2 Buy Vaseline 4 Moi."

5. "La Bamba," by Ritchie Valens. According to Rodrigo the ABS lab tech, this classic of early rock-and-roll is a straightforward account of masturbating to a photo of Chita Rivera. Thanks, Rod!

A NOTE TO OUR READERS

While we at ABS hesitate to break the flow of your learning experience or possibly kill your wood, we find it necessary at this point to offer our readers an important disclosure.

We don't hide the fact that much of our research has been made possible by a substantial grant from MachoMax—a leading light in the Honduran herbal-supplement industry—and that, yes, in return for MachoMax underwriting such projects as this book and the ABS National Registry of Glory Holes (soon to be a handy iPhone app), we have agreed to provide endorsements of useful MachoMax products. Here are two, among many, that we can heartily recommend: Sex Titan Oil-Based Genital Slickener (*sic*) and Macho One-A-Day All-Herbal Vagina Enlargener (*sic*).

Though MachoMax agreed to a silent sponsorship and to leave writing books to us, the experts ("*los maricones*"), the CEO called two weeks ago from his Tegucigalpa office with some editorial suggestions. Some of these suggestions were troubling (e.g., that the graffiti tag of the most powerful street gang in Honduras be visible as an airbrushed backdrop in all author photos), but others offered good food for thought. And one in particular—the suggestion that we add a female researcher to our team—was a stroke of brilliance.

For a long time now, ABS has been a team of men's men. A wild and woolly crew, to be sure, bursting with testosterone, likely to "bro down like a hoedown" one minute and entwine a lovely female in an embrace of exquisite carnality the next. But let's face it: Our research-grant commitments aren't getting any younger. Heaven knows we love our clinic. It's part antiseptic shrine to the scientific method, part balls-out firehouse where boys can be boys—but it sure could use a woman's touch, especially when it comes to our ratty sofa in the ultimate-fighting room. It's as true in science as it is in life: Sometimes deep down, the lion wants—even *needs*—to be tamed.

So it's with enormous pleasure that we announce the newest member of our team: the brilliant and beautiful Dr. Allison Silverman. Dr. Silverman comes to us from none other than our crosstown rivals, the Society for Sensuality in Sex—a bunch of jerks if ever there was one, even if we do steal their wireless. With that said, we're putting past unpleasantness behind us. Dr. Allison Silverman—Allie to us—has made her choice. And it is ABS! Needless to say, we are walking on air, and soon you will be, too! Dr. Silverman, she's a hottie!

Greetings to My ABS Colleagues

By Dr. Allison Silverman

Thank you, gentlemen, and God bless America! I am so pleased to be talking to you about sex in this beautiful country.

I was not always so lucky. You see, I grew up in the Soviet Union, in a small Siberian smog-mining town called Yakutsk. When you say Yakutsk out loud it sounds like you are sneezing! But I hope you are not, because in Yakutsk, a sneeze will kill you. My younger brother once coughed and suffered irreversible liver damage.

Let's get serious. Sex was not easy under a Communist regime. As a child, I remember holding my mother's hand as we stood in line for hours just to rub against a worn piece of felt. Frequently, the encounter would end awkwardly, with the felt refusing to accept a tip. It was not until years later that we learned how many of these "pleasure felts" had once held prestigious positions at universities—that is, until they published scholarship that was critical of the Kremlin.

I do not wish to paint too dreary a picture! After years of bargaining with the State Inspectorate, my father successfully exchanged a scratched Lionel Richie album for entry into a communal apartment. We divided everything equally with our housemates, and I was frequently the recipient of a twelfth of an orgasm.

Thanks to my brother's liver damage, he skipped two grades in our local academy for the development of future alcoholics. I was not so lucky. As a teenager—when I should've been learning to repair coolant pumps at the local nuclear-power station—I found myself beset by a series of accidents. First my breast buds blossomed. Then I unfolded like a delicate orchid. Before I could recover, I ripened into full flower. And finally, I had a dream that I was nursing a unicorn while Anatoly the bus driver gave it to me doggy-style.

This is why, when the Society for Sensuality in Sex (SSS) participated in a cultural exchange program with our Workers' Committee for the Enhanced Lovemaking of the People, I traveled all the way to Moscow from my small town, hundreds of kilometers away. As the festivities came to a close, I hid in the Society's six-foot condom intended to illustrate the mythic prophylactic of the Greek god Peniculus. Before long, I was in my new home, America.

I tell you my story so you will take advantage of what this magnificent nation offers your sex life: capitalism. Only when I saw America's wealth did I realize how Communism had stunted my understanding of pleasure. Believe it or not, I had never even met a man rich enough to have two families who are unaware of each other! Yet here it is an everyday luxury. You see, in the Soviet Union, no matter how hard you worked, you had the same sex as everyone else, so there was no way to know whether you enjoyed it. Here, with a little ambition and financial know-how, you can come home to your penthouse every night and know that you have the classiest sex in the building. It is just a matter of initiative. Consider Andrew Carnegie, the son of a weaver, who immigrated to the Unites States and made hundreds of millions of dollars in the steel industry. It is hard to imagine how much better his orgasms were than his poor parents' in Scotland!

Some say that sex is life's one great free pleasure. I would like to take them back to Yakutsk. And put them in a unicorn costume, while Anatoly the bus driver gives it to them doggy-style.

HEY, DIDJA KNOW...

By law, citizens in Switzerland are only permitted to masturbate twice a year—so they *really* have to make each time count?

The strangest thing ever masturbated to is a box of Cinnamon Toast Crunch?

Guys named Kip masturbate three times longer than average?

A man who ejaculates forcefully enough can impregnate the cosmos?

Masturbation is one of two sexual acts for which you can earn an online associate's degree (the other is advanced frottage)?

CHAPTER 6

FETISH, DOMINATION, AND MULTIPLE SEX PARTNERS

(FORMERLY "THE SEXUAL HABITS OF U.S. SENATORS")

Everything we've discussed up to this point has dealt with what you might call "vanilla" sex —conventional non-freakiness that can be enjoyed by nearly everyone with waterproof flooring and stain-resistant slacks. You really could stop reading here and be fine. Actually, nature kind of *meant* for you to stop here and be fine. But the human imagination is inexhaustible, and why should we expect the creative vision that invented astronaut ice cream and God to settle for standard penis/vagina fare? Once you have the basics down, you'll find there's a whole world of erotic variations for you to explore—all it takes is an open mind and a junior-high-school (or equivalent) education.

Take fetishes, for example—sexuality's big tent. Show a man with a shoe fetish a woman in high heels, and he will drop to his knees to kiss the patent leather. Remove the shoe, and a foot fetishist will jump in to worship every little piggy on that most intoxicating of extremities. Remove the foot and an acrotomophile stands ready to pay tribute to that heavenly absence, the amputation. In fact, there isn't a body part, inanimate object, or idea that someone hasn't found a way to eroticize—one person's excuse to park in the handicapped spot is another person's masturbatory temple.

No overview of fetishes would be complete without a more thorough look at the most popular of them all: domination-and-submission. If you've ever been strapped to a crucifix and flogged for ejaculating before Mistress ordered you to, you're what's known as a submissive, the subservient partner in this sort of power-exploitation relationship. On the other hand, if you've ever found yourself in your customized dungeon, sipping from a champagne flute as you penetrate a client with a series of increasingly wicked dildos and RCA universal remotes, you're what's known as a dominant. Not sure which one you are? You'll know by the end of this chapter, sissy.*

The final delight discussed in this chapter is sex with multiple partners at once, commonly referred to as "monogamy by committee" or "orgasm by the batch." While your friends and neighbors might publicly look down on this behavior, 63 percent of them indicated in an ABS survey that they and their partner had, at least once, arranged a casual get-together with a potential third lover at a Ponderosa Steakhouse equidistant from their homes. In almost every instance, the trio consummated the new acquaintanceship at a nearby motel, during which the man (or both men) complained about the air conditioner not working and ejaculated in under five seconds.

In short, with a little daring, sex doesn't have to be the stoic act of Depression-era penetration your grandparents constantly reminisce about. If you think you can handle something new, let us show you how.

FETISH:
WHATEVER TURNS YOU ON

The word *fetish* comes from the Esperanto word *femtachezera*, which, loosely translated, means "to gorge on a very specific melon from a secretly located patch." Just as every child has his or her favorite crayon in the box, we as adults have our favorite "crayon" in the bedroom—and sometimes that "crayon" isn't found in *any* box. Other times, it's an actual crayon.

For most of history, fetishes were dark, shameful secrets, and the dread of being exposed as someone who fancied a nontraditional bedroom experience drove many a fetishist underground. Secret societies were formed and quietly attracted an enormous following of millions who simply could not help themselves. The social groups Barons Who Sniff and Swains of the Turtle were, alone, believed to have accounted for one-third of all sexually active males in Elizabethan England.

Go on. Keep staring, pervert.

*We're just guessing here.

Times have changed, of course, but many of us still fear our fetishistic urges. Our goal at ABS is to eliminate shame from your bedroom (unless, of course, shame is your "thang") and help you embrace what turns you on, as long as it's not hurting others (unless that's their "thang"). Whether you love having your face sat on by a big ol' jiggly-wiggly gigantic bottom or dressing up as Marmaduke and getting your furry on, you now have a cause to celebrate.

Of course, that's not to say that one can't or shouldn't be discreet. A sense of discretion can certainly heighten, and even prolong, one's erotic experience. For instance, if you derive sexual pleasure from seeing Asian women pick up after their teacup Chihuahuas in your local park, it might behoove you to keep that to yourself and to simply stand back, watch, and enjoy. Yelling "We've got liftoff!" at the top of your lungs while clawing at the front of your denim shorts as she places her hand over a lump of excrement could severely limit future opportunities for gratification. To put it simply, in the words of Kenny Rogers: "You got to know when to hold 'em, and know when to" be afraid to publicly disclose your desire to masturbate.

Regardless, you should always be rejoicing inside, embracing whatever sexual idiosyncrasies you've been blessed with by the good Lord above. Because whether you're running your tongue along the floor of a Times Square peep booth while wearing nothing but a gunnysack or garroting yourself with Christmas tinsel, you're feeling something only *you* can feel. You're experiencing a pleasure that belongs to no one but *you*. And that is wonderful! What a gift!

SEXUAL ROLE-PLAY:
FETISH IN FUNNY HATS

Sexual role-play is a fun, inexpensive approach to exploring your fantasies with an all-too-familiar partner. Think of it as year-round Halloween that arrives whenever you're horny. Anything works within this fantastical world . . . or *almost* anything. For instance, pretending that you're a bored housewife who meets a fifty-year-old pizza deliveryman who still wants to make it big on the Swedish death-metal scene might not be terribly pragmatic. Furthermore, fantasizing that you're an illegal alien handling jobs that no one else wants, such as assisting farm vets in shaving down horses' testicles, probably isn't going to cut it, either.

After many years of scientific study, however, ABS has found that there are, indeed, a number of role-playing scenarios that are actually *guaranteed* to work:

- "Travelling Renaissance bard" meets "a young Roger Ebert"
- "Door-to-door Bible salesman" meets "a housewife who doesn't believe in God but does very much believe in man's capacity, even need, to withstand horrific, life-ending pain"
- "Former secretary of state Condoleezza Rice" meets "a midget porn star with a deep, fanatical interest in foreign policy"
- "Genghis Khan, one of the greatest adventurers who ever lived" meets "a cashier from Walgreens named Kathy"

Of course, this is all fairly conventional stuff, and maybe you're the kind of person who, after so many years, is finally unable to become seduced at the callused hands of a smooth-jazz vibraphonist without growing bored. Fortunately for you, there's an entire world of fetish you probably didn't even *know* existed!

"LITTERBOXING" AND OTHER HIGHLY RAREFIED SEXUAL FETISHES

Were it not for the Internet's extraordinary global reach, less common fetishes such as litterboxing (i.e., forcing one's cat to make prolonged eye contact while it performs its toilet, and then pleasuring oneself to the feline's expression of withering shame and humiliation) would never have experienced the popularity they enjoy today.

I CAN HAZ ORGZM?!?

TASCHEN

Before the Internet, this expensive book collection of feline-humiliation photographs would have been considered niche.

Although fetishism has become a largely accepted form of sensual expression, some rarefied sexual proclivities continue to lurk quietly along the shadowy fringes of human sexual behavior. There they remain, hidden, until some enterprising teenager in a high-school computer-science lab distractedly searches Google for "Howie Mandel + hand job + back of rented Geo + Baltimore + Band-Aid."

In order to find the absolute rarest of sexual fetishes, ABS has plumbed the depths of human perversion—from ultra-private Internet message boards to the "staff picks" section of a German Barnes & Noble. What we discovered astounded even us. Some of these fetishes have only a handful of practitioners; some have none. But who knows—any of these uncommon sexual obsessions could find its way into the mainstream and perhaps one day become as widely popular as a garden-variety Cabbage Patch Doll + miniature-prom-dress fixation (huge in Pennsylvania Dutch country).

Free-spacers

These fetishists seek a particular pleasure in rented halls and church basements, refusing themselves sexual release until the moment someone signals a winning card by shouting "Bingo!" (More orthodox practitioners will prolong their relief further, timing their orgasm only after the bingo win has been confirmed by a church officiant, preferably flown over from the Vatican.)

This noted entertainer and fetishist could only experience an erection with another man's hand inside him.

Marcel Marceaunanism

These finicky fetishists are repelled by all forms of physical intimacy, and can only achieve sexual release by watching someone else roll their eyes and sarcastically mime a hand job.

Animanthropomartiphilia

Projecting erotic fantasy onto animated figures is a practice as old as animation itself, and assigning human sexual characteristics to animals is as natural as deliberately setting fires to sublimate sexual desire. However, neither of these fetishes approach the rare taboo of animanthropomartiphilia—or an attraction to animated animals that resemble filmmaker Martin Scorsese.

A LITTLE OUT THERE:
NECROPHILIA, BESTIALITY, AND MISCELLANEOUS FETISHES

It's a founding tenet of ABS that all sex is good sex. From a four-man group grope in the cab of an eighteen-wheeler, enhanced by a playfully racist David Allan Coe album on the cassette deck, to the heartwarming pubescent fumblings of a budding dirty-sole fetishist, if it involves stiffening body parts and fleeting shame, chances are it's beautiful. Are you not quite sure where your sexual appetites fall on the spectrum between "exotic" and "damn, you nasty"? Then try employing our Concentric Circles of Porn Display psychological-profiling test. Generally speaking, the further the sexual paraphernalia that "does it" for you is stocked from the fireproof, lead-lined gun safe hidden under floorboards in the porn shop's back room, the less likely it is you'll be tackled by FBI agents upon checkout.

Illegally disgusting

Should be hidden from partner

Could talk your way out of it if discovered

Totally kosher

If your favorite adult videos are displayed against the far wall of the porn shop, beneath the canvas tarp, you may wish to turn to prayer.

The last thing we at ABS want to do is get all Judgey McJudge on those whose sexual interests strike us as a tad unusual. So rather than gainsay their preferences, let's hear from society's "special little monsters" themselves, in these testimonials submitted through the ABS website, OurBodiesOurJunk.org.

Necrophiliac, age 47

Sure, I understand that sex with the dead isn't everyone's bag. Quite frankly, though, I don't give a rat's patoot. I have a funny saying: "Keep your laws off my bodies." Ha ha! See? I have a terrific sense of humor. Most necrophiliacs do. I might spend the occasional evening waiting for crowds to thin out around the football-throwing body at the Body Worlds exhibit so I can masturbate spasmodically underneath my Old West–undertaker trench coat while humming the funeral march, but you, my friends, are bigots. Which is worse?

Flasher, age 18

The guys at school think I'm some kind of pervert for being so into flashing my penis and balls. There are only, like, two tables left in the cafeteria where I'm welcome to sit, and even at those, no one will look under the table anymore when I tell them something really interesting is down there. I'm banned from the American Girl Place, and that's hard on my little sister. Meanwhile, a lot of the other flashers I meet in chat rooms tell me I'm too young to flash. Sorry, I didn't know fiftysomethings were the only ones with penises no one wants to see. I'm being sarcastic. People suck.

Beast lover, age 22

First of all, I fuck dolphins. Would you call a beautiful, sleek, intelligent dolphin a "beast"? No? How, then, is it bestiality? Furthermore, is a porpoise a dolphin? Very nearly. So fucking porpoises is not really an issue, either, as we can all agree. Now, let's discuss marlins, who are remarkably similar in size and heft to one of your larger dolphin breeds. Of course—yes, I know!—a marlin is a fish and dolphins are mammals, but that is one for the ancient philosophers to ponder. Let's just agree it is okay to fuck marlins. Now let's talk about beached jellyfish. Stay with me here . . .

QUIZ: ARE YOU SEXUALLY ATTRACTED TO ANIMALS?

According to the PETA website, four out of every five adults are sexually attracted to animals or insects—but only three out of every five adults have acted upon it. For everyone else, bestiality is an unfulfilled desire, suppressed by fear or puritanical pet-store policies. If you wonder if perhaps you harbor an attraction to animals, take this quiz, specially designed to target the subconscious mind. It will help you to unlock any interspecies urges, as well as provide thorough instructions to help you perform your own quick and easy home castration.

1. With which historical figure do you most strongly identify?
   a. John F. Kennedy
   b. Joseph Stalin
   c. Lonnie Wheeler, inventor of the feline condom

2. Complete the following sentence: "Old MacDonald had a _____ ."
   a. cow
   b. pig
   c. dark and disturbing secret

3. If you could bottle the odor of sexuality, what would you call the perfume?
   a. Leather & Lace
   b. Fiery Flesh
   c. Recently Digested Oats

4. Which, if any, formative moment would you say contributed most to establishing your sexual identity?
   a. Discovering an old issue of *Playboy* on your father's night-stand
   b. Finding yourself aroused in your high-school locker room
   c. The first time you noticed Porky Pig wasn't wearing trousers

Most adolescent sexual awakenings are triggered by this half-nude cartoon pig.

Count the number of times you selected (c) in the questions above to determine your score:

0–1 Minimally, or not at all, aroused by animals. At most, an embrace with a llama will go a second longer than you're both comfortable with.

2 Some bestial urges, but nothing that can't be satiated simply by masturbating to the photo on a box of Meow Mix.

3 Strong zoophile tendencies. By now, pigeons know better than to approach your bread crumbs.

4 It is a testament to your incredible restraint that you would stop fondling an armadillo to complete this quiz. Good for you.

DOMINATION AND SUBMISSION:

TASTE THE WHIP! GO ON, TASTE IT!

Walk up to someone and ask them to describe the first vivid scenario that comes to mind when they hear the word *fetish*, and they'll probably describe a stern, corseted woman administering some sort of punishment to a man kneeling at her boots, leashed to a post or manacled to an oversize houseplant. And with good reason. So powerful, so iconic is the dynamic between a mistress and her thrall that domination-and-submission is a fetish that's truly a category in its own right. But if you don't know what you're doing, it's all too easy to find yourself among the thousands admitted to the hospital each year with conditions such as tether burn or obedience rot, both of which can easily turn you against domination-and-submission forever. For the information you require, keep reading.

A PRIMER FOR THE ASPIRANT LITTLE LORD FAUNTLEROY

You've just had sex. You've duly ejaculated inside the mutually agreed-upon orifice, and your partner, in full cuddling mode, moves in to spoon—and yet, you feel strangely unfulfilled. Why didn't she call you a worthless insect? Did she fail to electrocute your prostate, or were you just not paying attention? And the meat-tenderizer hammers—where were all the damn tenderizer hammers? If you find yourself mulling over these questions, you're probably not having your submissive needs met. You may want to explore your options for suffering.

An encounter with a mistress usually takes one of three forms:

Submission by Appointment

The most common BDSM arrangement. First, a mistress and her submissive set aside an hour or so each week for the ecstasy of pain and degradation.* While this can occur at a sub's home or office, more often than not it will occur at a specially appointed dungeon. At the high end, these can be fully stocked pain chambers, with Inquisition-caliber bloodletting devices, leather-upholstered face-sitting thrones, and nipple-torturing robots that work almost noiselessly; at the low end, a dungeon can be little more than a refrigerator box equipped with razor wire torn from a nearby junkyard fence.

Long-term Submission

In what's otherwise known as lifestyle slavery, the 170-pound pile of obedience you call a life belongs to Mistress 24/7. If she wakes you up at 4:00 a.m. because she wants you to give her a pedicure with a cactus stuffed in your mouth, you'd better be on the first train. If she texts you in the middle of a board meeting because it's time to shoot an indescribable YouTube video involving Raggedy Ann makeup and an inverted bowling pin, meeting adjourned. This is the real-deal immersive experience. Only true thumb-sucking weaklings need apply.

Speed Submission

Of course, long-term subservience requires tremendous chemistry between the mistress and her submissive—but who has time to go searching for that? We work nights, weekends, and straight through our lunch breaks now, and the days when we could duck out of the office for a quick human-trampoline session are long gone. Enter speed submission. Launched in the 1990s, speed sub is a unique way for would-be submissives to sample the abuse from a variety of potential dominatrices. In a typical speed-sub event, equal numbers of men and women spend just a few minutes together before a bell rings and the man crawls to his

---

*Usually an individual rate. Some mistresses offer a discounted group rate, which explains why visitors to ABS headquarters sometimes find the five of us in a pile, shackled to the same pommel horse.

next encounter. These encounters are entirely free-form and range from verbal belittlement to an abbreviated catheterizing session. At the end of the night, both men and women are given a card. The women mark an X next to the names of men they might consider receiving unflagging tribute from; the men's cards are immediately ripped apart and tossed in their faces. Hot appetizers and a house cocktail are typically included in the registration fee.

Speed submission is a fun, casual way to beg multiple mistresses for the healing power of their cruelty.

MISTRESS MAY I?
DOM DO'S AND DON'TS

The S/M slave's lot in life is a simple one: He lives only to please his mistress, and maybe to finally track down that rare leather-and-steel sack splitter that won't be visible under his golf pants. But before you sit down for even one more late-night nipple-destruction session in front of the webcam, take a moment to look over the following hints.

1. **SHE'S YOUR SLAVE MASTER, NOT YOUR MOTHER.**
    Plenty of men use the dungeon as a place to work out long-simmering resentment toward their parents, but if you've got issues, don't expect Mistress to pass the tissues. She wants to know that the blubbering you're doing is because of her rapid-fire flamenco stomps on your scrotum, not because of the pants-down spanking Mommy once administered in front of your PeeWee football team. Sack up, butt boy!

2. **RESPECT THE LEASH.** We can't tell you how many times we've shaken our heads in embarrassment watching some overzealous dog-boy yank his poor mistress hither and yon, hither and yon around the dungeon floor. Hey, who's walking whom here, fop? The same rule applies for cock leashes.

3. **TRY BEFORE YOU BUY.** "All whipping posts are alike. I'll just add one at random to my online shopping cart and go about my dirty, dirty business." Famous last words, slave! Is your pain-play better served by a standard six-foot flogging pole with adjustable swivel shackles and spray-down polyvinyl mess gutters, or by a specialty product like MachoMax-brand Greedy Baby Convertible Whipping Station/Hoagie Stand? Think, you mewling worm-child!

4. **HEEL.** We said heel, you mardy-assed little toerag!

5. **DON'T FORGET TO NETWORK.** It's no secret that sadomasochism attracts the rich and powerful. That prosperous-looking gentleman with fishing weights hung from his penis at the next stockade over might just have a job for an enterprising young slave like yourself. Fact: 90 percent of executive search ads in *The Economist* would not have been necessary if only somebody had taken the trouble to pass a business card between tightenings of the ball clamps.

SAFE WORDS: THE WORD OR PHRASE THAT MAKES HER TAKE THE BOOT OFF YOUR THROAT

The nature of BDSM sex play makes it necessary to have a word or phrase other than "Stop!" or "Help!" or "For Chrissake, no!" Something is needed to firmly draw the line in the sand: "I've had enough, I'm not playing around any longer, this time *no* does actually mean no." Often, the best choice is one that falls far outside normal sex talk—which is why "Harder," "More suffocate-y," and "Wake up, Mr. Sizemore" make terrible safe words. After extensive hands-on research here at the ABS-fetish linguistics center, we have concluded that by far the easiest and most effective safe word is "Murphy." It is easy to remember, easier to say, and most importantly, the sounds of the word are made primarily in the front of the mouth, making it much easier to utter when the airway is restricted or the larynx is being slowly crushed by an anvil.

Other Effective Safe Words:

Rhubarb

Mudslide from Applebee's

1978 Detroit Lions

Mrs. Nussbaum's credit card

Eatin' soft-shell crabs at the Maryland Shore

Darius Rucker

Hooker, you fat

I went to Camp Sea Gull in North Carolina

Winkus-Dinkus

Otis Spunkmeyer's raw dough

When the pawn hits the conflicts he thinks like a king
What he knows throws the blows when he goes to the fight
And he'll win the whole thing fore he enters the ring
There's no body to batter when your mind is your might
So when you go solo, you hold your own hand
And remember that depth is the greatest of heights
And if you know where you stand, then you'll know where to land
And if you fall it won't matter, cuz you know that you're right

CHOOSING THE PERFECT INTERIOR DECORATOR FOR YOUR BASEMENT DUNGEON

It's not easy being a perfectionist . . . especially if you're in an occupation as high-pressure and wildly unpredictable as beating and whipping white-collar workers during their lunch breaks in your converted S/M basement dungeon.

Let's not lie: It is *extremely* important to you that everything looks and feels *just right*. Then again, you don't necessarily want to buy into what Mr. and Mistress Jones down the street consider the latest word in S/M refinement. This is why it helps to hire an outsider—an expert at taking something drab, pedestrian, and "useful" and transforming it into something so glamorous and beautiful that snapshots will be taken and then proudly hung on the walls of delis as advertisements for local photographers.

The first thing to consider when choosing an interior decorator for your dungeon is *taste*. In other words, do the both of you share the same interest in style and sensibility? Do you prefer a Colonial approach, while your decorator prefers a more modern take? There is no right or wrong answer. Just please keep in mind that fuck furniture and other bondage furnishings are available in practically every design style imaginable: shabby chic, retro, contemporary, art deco, Victorian, and even indigenous Mexican American folk art!

Another factor to consider is *affordability*. Sure, just about everyone dreams of owning a custom-made basement sex pit; who wouldn't? But can you really afford to build one? More importantly, will you ever be able to find a contractor who will be considerate of your living arrangements?

In other words, construction noise, combined with dirt and power tools, do not mix well with children, pets, and cranky gimps. The trick, if there even is one, is to hire a professional designer who is not only affordable but who'll be able to successfully juggle your alternative lifestyle with the fact that your kids will need to use the basement from time to time to host sleep-overs.

Here's something else: make sure that your decorator is not ashamed to go off-brand. When purchasing ass-spreaders, leather body bags, metal restraints, hitching rings, riding crops, Shur Shot kits, buckling rubber straps, and fur-lined blindfolds, there is no shame in purchasing them at Target as opposed to, say, Bloomingdale's. When you are stripped bare and receiving a "medical examination," will you be at all concerned that the black nitrile gloves inserted up your anus don't have a fancy Adidas symbol on each finger? Or that the linen adult diapers are Juicy Lucy and not Juicy Couture? You shouldn't be, and neither should your decorator.

Last, when looking to make your bizarre dream a disturbing reality, always choose a professional who is not afraid to "go green." Did you know that the Mustang Sally Doggy-Style Bench can be created with found items, such as driftwood and abandoned grocery carts? And did you realize that the Giddyup Leather Bondage Booth can be purchased "pro-cow" and "cruelty free"? And that the Mother May I Spanking Horse is fully recyclable and can now be accepted for pickup on Tuesday and Thursday mornings when dumped in front of a neighbor's curb?

A good interior decorator for your basement dungeon will not be easy to find, but the search will be well worth the effort. After joining forces, you and your new friend will accomplish the impossible: creating that dungeon basement you've been dreaming about since first falling in love with the charming, marvelous lifestyle as depicted in the great Garry Marshall masterpiece *Exit to Eden*. Dreams do come true.

BUILDING YOUR OWN SEXETERIA

If a basement dungeon is a little too much (just a little *too* nouveau riche) and your interests lie more with casual sensual play, why not just turn your house's guest room into a sexual playground—or sexeteria? Most couples find that their erotic-fetish-on-a-budget can easily be produced with only one small room and less than 1,000 in Marlboro Miles.

Use this room diagram and sexual-equipment cut-outs to arrange the floor plan of your own affordable personal sexeteria. Enjoy!

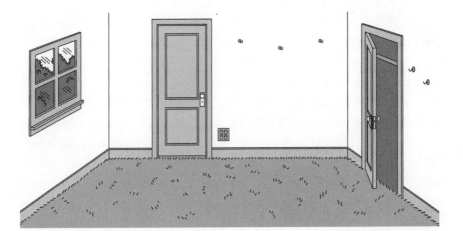

Big Mouth Billy Bass, the Singing Sensation

Adult-sized squirrel costume

Zipper mask

"Sybian" La-Z-Boy with inset hydraulic dildo

Mini-fridge stacked with Mike's Hard Lemonade

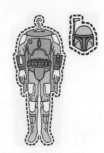

Boba Fett costume

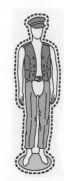

Wilson leather and suede brand "Leather Daddy Caddy"

Twin mattress with polypropylene wee-wee cover

Can of Glade (Island Escape™ scent)

Nintendo Wii

Tupperware bowls filled with mini-pretzels and fun-size Baby Ruth candy bars

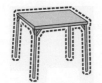

Folding bridge table

19th-century teakwood vibrator display case

Stack of *Oui* magazines

SEX WITH MULTIPLE PARTNERS:

ORGASM WITHOUT BORDERS

Opening up your relationship to physical intimacy with others is an excellent way to introduce some novelty into a sex life plagued by loyalty and commitment. Some couples reach a point where they need to break away from the familiar for the thrilling newness provided by swap-and-roll karaoke night at a swingers' club called Chateau Wet. But many couples settle for the status quo, night after night barely getting by on rote copulation with a lover whose kiss is bland and predictable, and whose genitals are out of fresh surprises. They'd rather live a life of erotic listlessness than be one of "those" people. Well, we at ABS are five of "those" people, and we say you're missing out.*

NEGOTIATING YOUR THREESOME, THE NO-TEARS WAY

If you're a woman, arranging a three-way sexual encounter between yourself, your partner, and another woman is as hassle-free as it gets. For starters, you can simply ask your partner to write out the running list of candidates he's been keeping in his head since the moment your relationship began. Then go through the list together, crossing off women you aren't both attracted to, who live too far away, or who rate as insufficiently freaky-deaky. Don't feel as if you have to tackle the entire list in one sitting! Such lists are often very long and heavily annotated.

---

*In truth, more than a few of us at ABS are not allowed within five hundred yards of group sex.

If you're male, you might have some serious wheeling and deal-ing ahead of you. If you're lucky, your partner considers herself bisex-ual—not in the sense that in her exclusive monogamous relationships she alternates between men and women, but as a free spirit known to invite attractive strangers to join you at erotic barbecues. At the very least, she's hinted that she isn't rigidly hetero. Maybe she's made passing reference to experimenting in college, or off-handedly sug-gested that you depilate your chest and tuck your genitals between your thighs until she's once again prepared to face her hetero prison.

Be aware that even if your partner consents to a threesome in principle, she will want control over the setup—particularly with sexual boundaries. For example, you may be forbidden from climax-ing inside the other woman or only be allowed to ejaculate into the crook of her knee. In fact, don't be surprised if your first threesome is far more chaste than you'd like—sometimes it takes at least six or seven encounters worth of quiet, nonsexual hair braiding before the necessary trust is established. Whatever restrictions you agree on, it's essential that all three of you discuss them in advance. Nothing kills the mood quite like stopping to recall that conversation seven frozen margaritas ago that concerned which orifices are on the "whatever's clever" list.

Unfortunately, it's possible your partner will simply have no in-terest in welcoming another woman into her bed. But that's okay. There's more than one way to get to three.

GUY-GUY-GIRL: THE GOLDEN RATIO

Slandered viciously as "the devil's threesome" or "the poor man's gang bang," a ménage à trois between two gentlemen and one lady is actually the most beautiful and misunderstood of all sex acts. While some of the practices described in this chapter are, to say the least, not for everyone, the same cannot be said for guy-guy-girl threesomes. They are indeed for everyone.

Perhaps you've found yourself having sex with a partner and thinking, *Something is missing here—something profound and alive that would fill this terrible emptiness.* You'd be forgiven for thinking that that "something" is love. In fact, it's probably just a second dude. There's no sex that can't be improved upon by the presence of another man at the foot of the bed, crouching naked while he sips an Amstel Light and waits to be tagged in. The aroma of his sport-scent deodorant. His subtle grunts as he registers approval for each of your thrusts. His kind offer when the delivery boy arrives with the Mexican food: "Don't worry, I got that. Y'all just keep fuckin'."

Two-person sex is like a classical pianist accompanying the soaring vocals of an opera diva: a pleasant enough soundtrack for picking out a blazer at Nordstrom's, perhaps, or waiting for periodontal surgery. But add some bottom end—courtesy of a movin', groovin' slap-bass player with a cool pair of shades and a big ol' funky grin—and now you've got music, Jack! Granted, some people may initially balk at the idea of inviting in the slap-bass player. These quibbles could come from either gender.

What he's thinking:

Is she going to keep calling me "boss man" like she did in the getting-to-know-you phone call?

What she's thinking:

His personal ad sure used the words "throwing star" a lot.

Misgivings like these should be taken very seriously, then washed into oblivion with five or six tumblers of Crown Royal blended whisky moments before the sex begins.

Many couples plan for the complications that may arise during guy-guy-girl lovemaking by agreeing on an opt-out clause that can be invoked at any time. This is fine, perhaps even wise, but make sure you share the information with your gentleman caller. The members of ABS speak from experience: nobody wins when some knock-kneed househusband decides at the last minute that he's not ready to run with the big dogs, and the helpful stranger from Craigslist has no choice but to pack away his Trojan Grope 'n' Go Travel Pak and finish himself off on an unfamiliar back porch.

SWINGING: WHAT YOUR MAILMAN IS REFERRING TO WHEN HE ASKS IF YOU PARTY

Swinging is the practice of swapping sex partners, often in a party atmosphere, usually in a suburban basement owned by a man who's excited to show you the Rolling Rock taps he just installed by the utility sink. While the popularity of swinging has fluctuated since the 1970s (when it was considered an acceptable activity, even for golden-anniversary parties and March of Dimes "Fun-Raisers"), today it's estimated that thousands—possibly even millions—of American couples love to swap. Perhaps even all.

The swinging lifestyle (or just "the lifestyle," as your bank teller knowingly refers to it) is so popular that stereotyping the typical swinger is pointless, except for the fact that most swingers tend to be middle-aged men pressuring their terrified wives to "loosen the hell up, we already paid for the harlequin masks." Let's not be coy: The reader has undoubtedly experienced the lifestyle for him- or herself, and is possibly even browsing this book during a chips-and-salsa break after watching the local P. F. Chang's manager bulldoze an unexpectedly well-toned school librarian. But, for the sake of argument, let's pretend that you don't already know.

Yes, even your bank teller likes to swing.

Perfect for a rainy day at the group beach house

These days most swingers meet online, on websites like Adult-Friendfinder.com and DrudgeReport.com (e-mail the editors of the latter for secret locations of sizzling-hot fuck parties in your area—they'll play dumb at first, but keep the pressure on and eventually they'll share their secrets). The initial step in using these websites (after coping with the disappointment that your preferred username, HubbySoHornyInMaryland21, has already been taken) is finding a couple with whom you and your partner have chemistry. Though in real-world, person-to-person interactions establishing chemistry is a complicated process taking into account everything from physical appearance to educational background and even genital scent, on-line it is typically a matter of deciding if you can live with "6.5 inches cut" even though your profile clearly stipulates "7 inches minimum and yam-shaped."

Group of single "lost boys," shortly before crashing a perfectly good sex party

The icebreaking process between swapping couples can be extremely delicate. In the 1970s, it usually began with one couple inviting over another for a night of lawn darts and Super 8 mm pornography. Late in the evening a wife would compliment her neighbor's husband on his fashionable turtleneck dickey, thus signaling the swap should commence. Things aren't so simple these days, but a low-key get-together is still recommended, encompassing jolly banter, shared nakedness, and a fun icebreaker game or two (we suggest investing in Cranium: Butt-Naked and Polyamorous Edition).

If you plan to swap in a party or club atmosphere, be aware that these gatherings almost always operate according to a strict set of rules:

1. **NO SINGLE GUYS! EVER! CAPICHE?** That means you, Mr. Lonesome! There are very few places where lonely single men are truly welcome, and swingers parties are no exception. Too many elegant swinger affairs have been made awkward by the lingering presence of single male interlopers (or "lost boys," as they're known in the lifestyle). That fortysomething, married media CEO gently guiding a stranger's feet into the "Scrumpin' Swing" stirrups worked hard to carve out his niche in society—you will respect his fantasies.

2. **PUNCTUALITY COUNTS.** Fashionable lateness is an unknown concept in the swinging world. Once a foursome install themselves atop the velvet-draped performance pedestal in the center of the grand ballroom, the last thing they want is to be interrupted by John and Judy Scatterbrain, bumbling in two hours late with a conciliatory bottle of prosecco.

3. **ALWAYS JOIN THE MAN POSSE.** Thinking of bringing drugs to a swinging party? Or getting embarrassingly drunk? Or breaking the concentration of everyone in the daisy chain with your personal drama? The 3 *D*'s of swinging misbehavior are punishable by immediate ejection from the premises by an ad hoc posse of partygoing males. When the posse comes calling, save your excuses, and don't bother tamping down your fully engorged penis. *It's go time, swinger!*

Of course, we don't mean to give the impression that swapping is all about a bunch of silly killjoy rules and regs. Aside from the above, the only real guidelines for swinging are:

1. Have fun.
2. Make love.
3. Try not to obliterate your marriage.

HOW TO CRASH AN ORGY

Contrary to what you might think, the best way to crash a stranger's orgy is to walk right through the front door, armed with all the confidence of Jay Leno at an antique-car show. If someone is standing in your way, dazzle him with one of the following lines as you smoothly brush past:

"Did you see the march for civil rights outside?"

"Don't worry about me—this boner is just for show"

"Is it cool if I remove my diabetic-socks for this thing?"

"Would you be a peach and fetch me a Sanka?"

"Just direct me to the game of ass-naked horseshoes, please."

"This is the best day after surgery ever."

Once you make your way inside the orgy site, you're more than halfway home. The trick is to be affable and charming but also inconspicuous. There is still a chance you'll be approached and questioned by someone who doesn't recognize you. If so, you'll need to have some additional lines ready:

"I hope you know you're talking to a tetherball champion."
A classic bait-and-switch, this line gets other attendees who may inquire about your presence, thinking, They have tetherball here? Or, in the case of confrontation by the host or hostess,

they will simply think you are talking about some advanced sexual technique and be shamed into silence—perhaps even tears—by their unfathomable ignorance.

"I'm a friend of Big Russ. Who are you?"

Count on it: At any swingers event, there will be an attendee nicknamed "Big Russ."

"Wait a sec—I gotta wear a rubber?"

If there's one thing that quickly diverts attention, it's putting people on the defensive. The beauty of this line is that no matter what answer you receive, you can react accordingly: relieved, bored, angry, baffled, bewildered, nauseated, catatonic, or drenched in sweat.

"Donna collapsed again. Have you seen her purse?"

This is alarmist behavior, yes, but it's also very effective in a pinch.

"Get in line. I got a lotta people to fuck and I ain't startin' with you."

This is perhaps the ultimate in false bravado, but if you embrace it, it works like a charm. Once you've mastered this attitude you will be able to tackle any stranger's orgy as if it were your own.

In the highly unlikely event that none of these lines works for you, you should have at least a few indispensable props close at hand:

Disco whistle.

Distracting and fun during sex.

Spark wheel and flash cotton.

An old wizard's trick. A must.

A blackjack or sap.

We're not advocating violence, but come on . . . you're technically trespassing.

Six thousand dollars in iTunes gift cards.

Bribes.

Falsified Make-a-Wish document.

This is a cheap ploy and should be used as an absolute last resort, but if you are in dire trouble, it will certainly melt the hearts of your aggressors to know that your dying wish was to attend what's-his-name's fuck fiesta.

Once safely at the orgy, be prepared to penetrate anyone and everyone with great haste. You may not have much time.

Farewell to My ABS Colleagues

From Dr. Allison Silverman:

Hello again, gentlemen of the Association for the Betterment of Sex. I have some exciting news! I am going to be rich!

Who would think that a girl from the Soviet Union could have such luck? In Yakutsk, it was considered good luck if you survived the winter.

As you know, I am an enthusiastic supporter of the free market and specifically of private investment in sexual research. In fact, much of my landmark work on clitoral dyslexia was done with the generous support of an anonymous benefactor named Wayne L. Gerard who lives with his wife, Kathy, in Newton, Massachusetts. That is why I was so impressed with the exciting investment opportunity offered to me by an up-and-coming researcher in the bathroom of a Pizza Hut. His name is Rob and he wants to reverse genital aging. For too long, men and women over the age of twenty-five have been plagued by withered, sagging genitals that look like a votive candle left under a heat lamp for too long. Rob's research suggests that a series of injections may be able to return these organs to their earlier shape! Onlookers will no longer mistake a mature vagina for Vincent Price in a funhouse mirror!

I invested my savings with Rob, and I owe him an additional $4.95 for the Diet Pepsi and bus fare. Once he finds a word to replace neurotoxicity, the procedure will take off and I will finally have the money for the sophisticated sex I've always desired! No longer relegated to the common mind-blowing orgasm, I will enjoy sensual pleasures previously known only to concertmasters in the world's finest philharmonics. I will indulge like the royals, and make love to my first cousin. I will bask in the urbane hand jobs of the yachting set.

I will be leaving the Association for the Betterment of Sex.

Yes, ABS, this is goodbye. Profits await and the horizon beckons. Thank you for your hospitality, gentlemen! You have treated me adequately. Until the money comes through, I am returning to the Society for Sensuality in Sex. They have promised me a new inkjet printer, and I intend to take them up on this most generous offer.

Пока!

Dr. Silverman, Don't Leave Us
...You Are Our Fair Russian Rose!

Dr. Silverman, as scientists and as men, we are devastated. You were with us for a short time, but as we huddle around our shared Dell laptop (remember how you would sweetly wipe the thick film of grime off the screen and call it "repulsive"?) and compose this missive, our memories spill over with the charming tales you told of your Eastern European homeland: how your family went to the bathroom in mine craters, how the television networks showed hard-core pornography in prime time, how you didn't think you could ever respect a man who hadn't at one time participated in torture. Beautiful stories. Enchanting as fairy tales.

Dr. Silverman—Dr. Allie—our only desire is to see you happy. And for you to never leave us. Ever ever ever ever. And for our rivals in SSS to suffer and die.

Stay with us. Please, Dr. Allie. For science's sake.

Yours,
The ABS team

HEY, DIDJA KNOW...

Many people applying for membership in NAMBLA complain about the invasive credit check?

The Marquis de Sade invented jeans?

Sixty-three percent of all girl-girl-guy threesomes end with the male prematurely ejaculating and then sitting alone in the kitchen drinking a Diet Sunkist?

The term "safe word" comes from the French phrase *savoir-faire*, meaning "tool belt"?

You lose about 200 calories during thirty minutes of sex, equal to the slab of fudge you just used as a lubricant?

Seven percent of people reading this book right now are unaware an orgy is going on just behind them?

CHAPTER 7

SAFE SEX AND CONTRACEPTION

PROTECTING YOURSELF FROM

DISEASE AND THE MIRACLE OF LIFE

Anything that's enjoyable comes with a risk attached. Think of that terrible hangover you experienced the day after the New Year's Eve party or the childhood home you burned to the ground while playing with Shabbat candles; if you're not careful, your fun can quickly turn against you. That's especially true with sex. Having unprotected intercourse against a urinal with that monster-truck mechanic just breezin' through town might at first seem like the most judicious thing in the world, but then there's hell to pay, the kind of hell that will make your crotch itch unabated for six months. Or, worse, the kind of hell that kicks at your womb.

Sexually transmitted diseases come in different forms—bacterial, viral, hypercolor—and range from the mildly lethal to the fatally irritating. In this chapter, we'll look at STDs as well as safe sex (the various killjoy measures available to minimize the risk of infection). By the time you finish reading, you will know everything necessary to make your lovemaking as fun and as sterile as a brand-new, unopened gauze pad.

We'll also explore contraception. While a baby is a blessing for partners planning to raise a family, it can be a blow for couples who might not be psychologically or financially prepared for parenthood, or who, according to prophecy, will conceive the Antichrist. Even in this day and age, many people don't know what methods of birth control really work. Too often a couple will find themselves staring dumbfounded at a pregnancy test and muttering something like, "I was sure we'd eaten the right amount of apple butter" or "That Gypsy insisted I was barren." This chapter will give you all the information you require to keep an unwanted child from entering the world.*

*Consult with your chosen house of worship to determine whether this is an abomination.

But we'll begin this chapter with . . . sigh . . . *abstinence*. Yes, it's the only fail-safe way to avoid STDs and pregnancy, but . . . who wants to live like that? Is that even living? Maybe we should stop *eating*, too. There's no salmonella in starvation, right? *Right?* Frankly, you should just skip this material. It will only pollute your mind.

ABSTINENCE:
THE SAD, PATHETIC SURE THING

Before you begin reading this section, you may want to send your genitals out of the room (just tell them that you hear something vibrating in the next room over). Abstinence—the practice of forgoing sexual intercourse, typically for religious, cultural, or fugly-related reasons—is no fun for anyone, least of all your penis or vagina. Yes, abstinence comes in handy for avoiding STDs or having something to chat with the older monks about while scraping beeswax out of the hive frames, but it will, without a doubt, make you the least popular visitor at any given Hedonism resort.

If you practice abstinence, your stay at Negril, Jamaica's Hedonism II resort will not be memorable.

The past decade has been exceptionally kind to abstinence, and we at ABS could not be more bothered about it. First President George W. Bush made abstinence-only education a cornerstone of his Third World foreign policy, demonstrating zero understanding that sex between desperate, sinewy Third World natives is the hottest and craziest sex around. Then American teenagers began signing "virginity pledges" and even trying against all common sense to "reclaim" their lost virginity, often in a madcap rush the night before high-school graduation (see the thoroughly unentertaining 2004 teen comedy *Regainin' It!*).

How to explain this madness? Is erotic self-denial really so fantastic? Nope, it isn't. When we tally up the list of the Ten Greatest Moments of our lives, it's hard to avoid the fact that at least seven of them involve inserting some part of ourselves into a part of someone else. True, abstinence offers ironclad protection against the following things:

1. Unwanted pregnancy
2. AIDS
3. Chlamydia
4. Syphilis
5. Gonorrhea
6. Genital herpes
7. HPV, scabies, pubic lice, head-to-toe pubic lice, so-called septic-crevice rot, and blah blah blah

But abstinence also has its share of negative consequences, not least among them:

1. Unnecessarily tidy house/apartment
2. Caring in the slightest about the emotional well-being of Clay Aiken
3. Clockwork-like monthly masturbation to the sex tips in *Redbook*
4. Long hours spent honing face-painting chops, trying to really nail "Dalmatian face"
5. Interest in the southern tradition of sacred music known as shape note singing (Quaker virgins only)

If you are considering embracing a celibate lifestyle, be sure to consult your doctor first. In fact, consider having sex with your doctor. Afterward, while collapsed in a clammy, panting heap in the supply closet where they keep the soiled scrubs and used sharps, ask yourself: *Could I ever really give this up?*

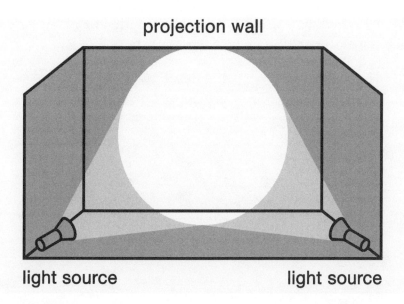

projection wall

light source   light source

SHADOW PLAY: HOW TO MAKE LOVE USING JUST YOUR SHADOWS

Shadow play (sometimes known as "dung puppetry") is a nice midway point between the fantasy of intercourse and actual intercourse, because while you *are* involved in an intimate act with another, you are also safely ensconced in your own space with no fear of physical interaction, or what OCD sufferers refer to as "human touchage."

The setup is relatively easy. Each person has their own light source, which they direct from their side of the room to a midpoint in the center of the wall in front of them. (See diagram.)

With a light source in each corner pointed toward the opposite wall, the beams will intersect halfway to that wall. (As you get more comfortable with your partner, you may wish to become slightly more intimate by using the same light source, preferably a tasseled bordello lamp.) The goal is to make your shadows intermingle, dance, and grab ass in all of the magnificent ways you would be able to if this were an actual physical lovemaking session instead of an infuriatingly unfulfilling charade. And what's wonderful is that there are actually *more* options in shadow play then there are in real lovemaking! (Ever made real love while a *T. rex* stands next to you and cheers you on? We doubt it.) The only thing holding you back is your imagination! Below are a few classic shadow-play positions:

1) GOIN' AT IT ON THE PINBALL MACHINE

2) I'M GALLAGHER, YOU'RE THE MELON

3) SOPHIE'S OTHER CHOICE

4) BRIAN WILSON'S MALAISE

MY PREFERENCE:
WHY I WEAR A PROMISE RING

By Jonah McCree, Abstinence Advocate

Whenever one of my teen peers first notices the gold filigree band encircling my finger, they'll usually ask, "Is that a wedding ring?"

"It's more like an 'up-until-my-wedding-ring,'" I'll respond with a wink. When they stare blankly, I'll add, "Let's just say this ring represents an important commitment I made."

"A commitment to being a total asshole," they often reply, punctuating the question with a strong shove to my chest. Once I'm able to catch my breath, I'll say, "If being committed to the Lord makes me an asshole, then I suppose that I am the *biggest* asshole in God's creation!"

To me, my very special ring represents three separate and equally important promises. The first promise is to Jesus, who died on a cross because teenagers were having vaginal intercourse before marriage. The promise ring is my way of letting Jesus know he doesn't have to pace around heaven, wondering if I'm having sexual relations. I'm not! Don't lose any sleep over me, Jesus! Go ahead and look the other way! LOL! There's no one in my bed except me, doing pencil sketches beneath my sheets and furiously erasing my mistakes. I make so many mistakes!

The second promise is to the special girls I meet in school, at church youth retreats, or at one of the many fun Christian online teen message boards, like Awesome-JC-Kool-Zone.org or TeenVibez.net. It is a promise that I will respect their purity. A promise that I will only give them a Christian side hug and not an intimate, secular front hug where our parts intermingle, straining against the fabric of our pants like an angry dog on a tether. A promise that when I ask any of these special girls to e-mail me a photograph, it's only so I can pray on them better, with a more accurate mental image. And a promise that when we're talking on the phone, if I become really quiet for a little while, it's only just because I'm taking a prayer break, and that rustling is merely the sound of my Bible pages shuffling, so you should just keep talking until I cry "Stop!" That's my ring's promise to you.

Finally, it's a promise to myself, to keep my body pure until marriage. Not an easy promise for someone who can basically have his pick of the litter. I don't mean to sound boastful, but in terms of basic teen sexual-attraction-determination factors, I am what one might call the "total package":

- I am first-chair clarinet in our school orchestra—only the third sophomore in our orchestra's history to hold that distinction.

- In my bedroom I have a Total Gym 3000, the highest non-professional-level Total Gym series, as well as a mini-fridge jam packed with Pöm brand pomegranate juice (retail: $4.85/bottle).

- I have an above-ground pool that's large enough for treading, floating, and light horseplay.

- This fall, my family is upgrading to Verizon FiOS high-speed Internet.

- While I suffer from cystic acne, I am currently under treatment and recently switched to a new, practically odorless face gel.

- My father owns That's a Wrap in the Potomac Village Shopping Center, and I am entitled to a friends-and-family discount of 15 percent on any regular menu items, including most wraps, paninis, and the brand-new organic Wrapinis.

Does possessing these qualities make it more difficult to preserve my chastity? Of course! But this challenge only strengthens my commitment! And does that mean I never feel tempted? Absolutely not, but I'll tell you what helps me get through those feelings of "straying from the flock": I just picture my future wife standing across from me at the church altar. And I think about what a great gift it will be to lead my bride to our marriage bed pure—absent any kind of prior sexual experience and free of even the most basic understanding of how to please a woman. And isn't that worth the wait?

SEXUALLY TRANSMITTED DISEASES:
WHERE LOVEMAKING AND BACTERIOLOGY MEET

Perhaps abstinence isn't for a free spirit such as yourself. The world is too tight and wet a place for you to wait for the person you'll spend the rest of your life with. You'll never be one of those married types who glumly looks upon her co-workers' twenty-person fuck helix and thinks, *Well, I had my chance, but I threw it all away for a year-long ride on the screw choo-choo.*

And yet, with that said, an assertively erotic lifestyle is not without risks, chief among them sexually transmitted diseases.

SEX WITH A JAUNDICED, GLASSY-EYED PROSTITUTE IS NOT WITHOUT ITS CONSEQUENCES

Allow us to introduce you to a very dear and special friend of the Association for the Betterment of Sex: our 66-year-old security guard, Howard Roberts. Or Robinson. Maybe Richardson. We're not sure.

Howie's in charge of many tasks around the ABS office, but his most important duty (by far) is to provide us with the most accurate, up-to-date point-spread for our weekly Redskins football pool. Howie then takes our cash, delivers it to a man we've never met and who supposedly works at Kemp Mill Records out in Wheaton, and then, after the game, informs us whether we've won or not. He's a tremendous asset to our team.

And yet Howie's not perfect by any means. Diabetes, concussions, and STDs have all taken their toll on this old-timer, and—as an obvious consequence—one can usually find the poor bastard off in the corner of our waiting area, warbling "Are You Lonesome Tonight?" to a life-size cardboard cutout of the late, great Spuds MacKenzie.

The reason we bring up Howie is that he loves prostitutes perhaps more than any other human alive.* Yes, there are serious risks involved with sleeping with a whore, sure, but there have *always* been certain risks inherent to just about anything that involves sticking your penis into the mouth or vagina of a dope fiend, pump jock, flatback harlot, midnight slummer, cock zombie, salt-chunk Mary, back-flip Betty, hoop queen, pavement princess, or puck bunny. Life is *jam-packed* with risks—which is exactly what makes it so damn exciting and rewarding to begin with!

Let us return to Howard—a great man, a wonderful husband, and a terrific father. The Howster served in Vietnam, earning himself the Medal of Honor. In his off time, this fella volunteers at Sibley Hospital, in the children's-cancer wing; he plays a juggling clown whom the kids simply adore. If the Howster wants to partake in some whorish fun, who are we to say otherwise?

Besides, what the hell does it matter anyway? Wouldn't you know it, but Howie's dead. Kind of murky on the where, why, and how much ABS is culpable, but all evidence (and a few YouTube videos) points directly to one pissed-off pimp prone to shanking those who insist on paying with hand-scrawled IOUs.

Funny, isn't it, how a man like Howie (who knew so very little, and who spent the majority of his time writing love letters to the Wizard of Id) could teach all of us so much? RIP, little man! Howard Rosenfeld, you will not be missed! Or Reynolds, maybe? Richards? Can't remember!

LESS WELL-KNOWN STDS

Every body part has its marquee afflictions. In the brain, it's Alzheimer's; in the lungs, it's bronchial gnomes. Our genitals also have their elite maladies, such as HIV/AIDS, syphilis, and chlamydia, among

---

*You're asking, "What guy doesn't love prostitutes?" Let's face it: all men pay for sex in one way or another anyway, right? Whether it's buying the wife an expensive dehumidifier for her "asthma" or pawning the outdated gaming system to purchase a nose job for the girlfriend, men are constantly doling out the dough for the dames.

others, and they've more than earned the distinction. But anyone who's sought a medical explanation for why their penis is behaving like a dowsing wand, or why their vagina is teaching itself card tricks when it thinks you're asleep, knows better. There's so much more that can go wrong.

Pubic wolves.

Pubic Wolves

Tiny predatory canines found in regions of pubic hair. The wolves travel in packs of up to a dozen, and can migrate from one set of genitals to another in a single act of intercourse. While not considered dangerous under ordinary circumstances, they can turn on their host's flesh when threatened or when pubic elk meat is scarce.

Scrivener Rot

Over the course of a couple of weeks to several months, a person contracting scrivener rot will lose the ability to transcribe, take notes, or certify documents. This malady was once the scourge of the promiscuous notary-public community, but educational outreach has since helped contain the epidemic.

Fourteen-karat Gonorrhea

A bacterial disease whose conspicuous feature is a glittering discharge that when collected and allowed to cool can be fashioned into bracelets by a skilled goldsmith. Usually fatal.

Reproductive Snow Camo

A mostly cosmetic condition that blanches the genitals to an arctic white mottled with black and gray splotches. Tests have shown that the camouflage offered by this condition is at least equally as effective as the alpine codpieces worn by special-forces soldiers.

Genital Scapegoating

For reasons still unclear to medical science, the private parts of individuals contracting this peculiar disease become objects of blame for all manner of personal problems and societal ills. Someone with genital scapegoating may not even know he or she has the disease until confronted by strangers with comments such as "Your vulva is why I drink" or "You know what's wrong with America? Your balls, that's what."

The disclosure of your disease is not the occasion for kitschy fun.

"HONEY, I'M HOME AND HIV-POSITIVE!": TALKING TO YOUR PARTNER ABOUT YOUR STD

There may be no less comfortable conversation to have with your lover than the one wherein you reveal that your genitals are the Rock-and-Roll Hall of Fame of communicable disease. And unlike the conversation about having a second family in Nevada, or the reasons the yakuza keep trying to run you off the road, this one can't be put off indefinitely. As difficult as discussing your STD might be for you, however, it's simply unfair to turn to your partner many years into your relationship and say, "Remember how we made love in the dunes that first time? That's why you're gradually going blind."

But, jeez, who wants to talk about that, especially since there's no guarantee your partner will buy you ice cream as a reward for your honesty? If it's any consolation, this important talk doesn't have to be the ordeal you think it will be, providing you approach it the correct way—the indirect way.

You can test the waters by presenting your partner with escalating hypothetical situations. Start with something like "My friend Danielle bought her fiancé a sweater he didn't like, but the store wouldn't take it back. What do you think he should have said?" If your partner offers a rational, understanding response, then gently steer the hypothetical toward the actual situation you're in: "What if I were Danielle, you were the fiancé, the sweater was herpes, and the no-return policy on the sweater was the lack of a cure for herpes?" If your partner says something conciliatory—"I'd be proud to wear that sweater every day, even if it's a metaphorical sweater representing an actual real-life disease you have afflicted me with"—you might then reveal the truth.

But most people aren't so quick to understand. Your revelation will come as an ambush and a betrayal, and no amount of offering to do the dishes for a month will make up for the fact that your partner's reproductive organs might soon turn to dust. Instead of just lumbering in with the information, you have to first lay some groundwork. Use everyday conversations with your partner to gradually prepare him or her for what's to come, and to frame it optimistically.

- "Honey, sometimes I'm just amazed at how well gonorrhea responds to antibiotics."
- "Nowadays, you can't walk ten feet without bumping into a way to make urination not feel like a flow of magma from hell itself."
- "Pass the marmalade. Also, AIDS isn't the death sentence it used to be."

If you're too squeamish to discuss the STD in even the most generic terms, there are plenty of more tortured ways to go about breaking the bad news. Ask your partner's boss to do it, for example, or leave a trail of rose petals leading to a pamphlet put out by the Centers for Disease Control and Prevention. Methods such as these, though, should be your very last resort. More likely than not, your partner will throw the personalized "Because of Me, You're Going to Go Insane with Syphilis" M&M's in your face and never speak to you again.

As undesirable as sexually transmitted diseases are, there are certain symptoms they will never produce. They won't gnaw at your nipples for nourishment, and they won't leave you to contend with a diaper full of unbelievably horrifying excrement three times a day. STDs may be a lot of things, but they're not babies. They do, however, have this much in common with babies: you get stuck with one the same way, and they don't really go away after eighteen years, like you'd hoped.

PREGNANCY:
MYTHS AND FACTS

Think fetuses are stupid? Think again. From time immemorial these barely alive clumps of human cells have been sneaking past our most ingenious defenses, directly into our wombs and—soon enough!—our pocketbooks. Short of installing a laser trip wire in our cervix, or hiring a retired police officer to sit in our bedroom and keep an eye out, no sperm-blocking method is 100 percent effective. But arm yourself with enough knowledge and you'll soon be sending the following message: *Hey, fetus! Go gestate someplace else! Got it? Thanks.*

MYTH: If I do not have an orgasm during sex, I cannot get pregnant.

FACT: Get real. Female orgasms are the stuff of campfire tales and crypto-zoology. If you believe this one, we've got a box of Bigfoot-skin condoms we'd like to sell you!

MYTH: I can't get pregnant if I have sex underwater.

FACT: Whether it's surf or turf, as long as sex involves a man ejaculating inside of a woman, pregnancy can occur absolutely anywhere—unless the man wisely intercepts his own sperm with a pool skimmer. So, yes, if you have sex in a pool with a reliable skimmer handy, *maybe* you're in the clear. We'll concede you that much.

MYTH: I can't get pregnant if I have sex in a theme-park wave pool.

FACT: What did we say? *Having sex underwater doesn't help!* Besides, you're probably thinking of the log flume. It's impossible to get pregnant during a steep descent or deadfall. Something to do with gravity.

MYTH: I can't get pregnant from pre-ejaculate.

FACT: We thought this was the case, too, but then we met our buddy, Tony, who was indeed conceived from pre-ejaculate. And it haunts him every goddamn day of his life. "Tony Pre-Cum," we call him. Sad.

MYTH: Sperm dies once it hits the air. Oxygen kills it.

FACT: Nope. The only way to kill sperm is to ejaculate directly into a cauldron of boiling oil or lukewarm acid.

MYTH: I can't get pregnant from anal sex.

FACT: Don't just take our word on this one: check out the all-anal episode of Discovery's *Mythbusters*. The guys do an experiment involving three thousand ball bearings and a crash-test dummy that clears things up pretty definitively.

MYTH: A sperm cell traveled far from its homeland in Greece on seas dangerous and strange. Captured by pirates, the sperm changed itself into a lion and chased the crewmen. When some of these crewman attempted to escape by jumping overboard, the sperm changed them into dolphins.

FACT: This one bears a striking resemblance to the ancient Greek myth of Dionysus, and sounds improbable. Never rely on a sperm's magical powers of transmogrification to prevent pregnancy.

By now you might be wondering if sex is even worth the risk. Maybe you'll just masturbate or channel your urges into performing at angry poetry slams like all the rest of your buddies. Well, relax. Sex may present risks, but there are *plenty* of ways to protect yourself. Just ask our friend, the condom. Or the pill. Or the pubic hairnet.

WEARING YOUR CONDOM CORRECTLY

When used properly, the average condom will ably withstand the friction of standard intercourse.* But while condoms rarely fail, their users often do. ABS research has found that a scant 18 percent of men successfully roll a condom onto their penis on their first try.† Even after half a dozen attempts, some men still fail to unfurl the condom, leaving a disc of latex stuck to their penis tip like a puny prophylactic shield. Instead of learning from their disgrace, many men simply fall into bad habits that they replicate throughout their sexual lives.

So let's start from scratch. There are four basic rules:

1. **MAKE SURE YOU'RE ACTUALLY USING CONDOMS.** If you find your condoms consistently unravel into rainbow nylon streamers, it's because you've been using wind socks. Granted, a very common mistake, but be careful.

2. **MAKE SURE THE CONDOM HASN'T EXPIRED.** An expired condom is likely to snap, disintegrate, or attempt to use you as a medium to communicate with a still-living loved one. Most condoms have the expiration date printed right on the wrapper. Some have an 800 number you have to call to get detailed information, and a few can be dated to only within a couple of centuries by comparing them with other artifacts originally buried nearby.

3. **REMOVE YOUR SPORTSWEAR.** Putting on a condom requires precision finger work that's impossible while wearing golf or batting gloves.

4. **DON'T DRINK TO EXCESS.** If you're highly intoxicated, you might lack the fine motor skills necessary to manipulate a condom. If that's the case, ask your partner to roll it on for

---

*Defined as 80-100 thrusts per minute, including up to three pauses to delay orgasm or to shove a cat off the bed.

†In the remaining 82 percent of cases, the condom ended up torn (42 percent), ingested (19 percent), at the bottom of a well (12 percent), on a neighbor's penis (8 percent), or skewered upon a restaurant-check spindle (1 percent).

you. Or, if she's equally inebriated, call a sober friend or, better yet, have a designated friend on standby in the basement. Do not call 911 for assistance. This is not an emergency. Use the standard police number and expect to wait up to half an hour.

THE SEXUAL SUBTEXT OF CONDOMS: FROM SCUMBAG TO SCHOLAR

If all condoms technically perform the same function—catching ejaculated semen and conveniently storing it for later use—then why are so many varieties available? Well, believe it or not, the condom you choose can communicate a great deal to your lover about the type of person you are.

Wonder what your condom says about you? Stop this instant—we've sorted it out.

CONDOM TYPE	WHAT IT COMMUNICATES TO YOUR LOVER
Standard latex	"Can you believe our RA had a whole mess of these in a plastic jar outside his dorm room? It's like he *wants* us to fuck."
Non-lubricated	"The only thing I care less about than my own pleasure is yours."
"Magnum" or extra-large	"My therapist says I have a problem with hubris."
Lambskin	"If given the choice, I would much rather have AIDS than a child."
"Rough Rider" studded/ribbed	"I make most of my family-planning decisions in truck-stop restrooms."
Flavored	"I have been told I'm incredibly considerate by more than one prostitute."
Colored	"I think sex should be an experience that is both disturbing *and* beautiful."
Female condom	"Look . . . a whole skid of these fell off the back of a truck on my way into work, nearly killing me. So let's just make the best of a bad situation here, okay?"

THE ULTIMATE CONTRACEPTION CHART

EFFICACY RATED 1 TO 5 DEAD SPERM—5 BEING THE BEST

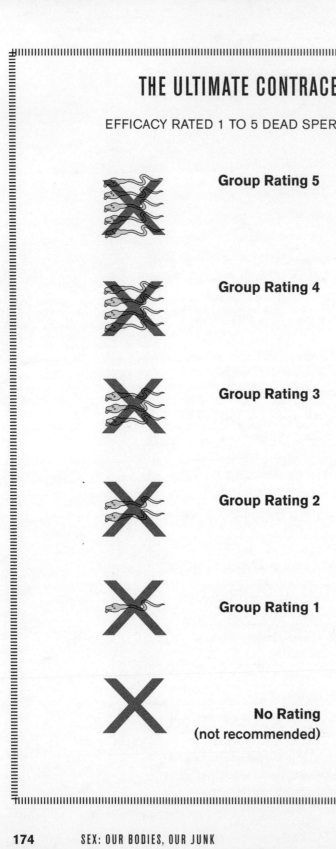

 Group Rating 5

Abstinence
Condom
The pill
Vasectomy

 Group Rating 4

The sponge
Vaginal ring
IUD
Morning-after pill
Fallopian knot

 Group Rating 3

A glandular stent
Gravy bouncer
Capitol Steps
Labian bodyguard

 Group Rating 2

Having your penis "turtled"
The testicular gooch
Superballin'
Mouse in the house

 Group Rating 1

Dad clamps
Koji's Revenge
Shrimp farm

No Rating
(not recommended)

Ice pants
Gutter slugs
Indigestion wheel
Penis in Lucite salad tongs

HOLISTIC CONTRACEPTION: PLUGGING YOUR PENIS WITH WITCH HAZEL AND OTHER POPULAR METHODS

The holistic-medicine industry—the reason you once gave yourself an enema with apple-cider vinegar after eating a half-pound of parsley—claims that birth-control pills throw women out of sync with Mother Nature in a way that's dangerous and unhealthy. We at ABS have always worked on the cutting edge of alternative healing (need we even remind you that we were first on the bandwagon for the whole rubber-band-as-a-treatment-for-lackluster-ejaculation-range fad?), and we think that the following all-natural, homeopathic contraceptive alternatives are worth your consideration.

This man uses holistic contraceptive methods.

1. **PLUGGING YOUR PENIS WITH WITCH HAZEL.**
   Is it uncomfortable? You betcha. Does it work? Jury's still out on that one! But Tigerman, the artist who panhandles outside the National Gallery with the "Ain't gonna lie—I'm usin' it for weed!" sign, really swears by it.

2. **SPERMICIDAL POMEGRANATE ICED BLACK TEA BY HONEST TEA.** Says so right there on the label!

3. **ANOINTING SACK AND GLANS WITH SUNFLOWER-SEED OIL.** This method is a favorite of Ayurvedic healers. Promotes balance in all things, and can be performed on the spot by most Indian-restaurant kitchen staff.

4. **WAVING A CENSER OVER YOUR GENITALS.**
   Obtain a censer—the swinging incense burner used in the Roman Catholic mass—and dangle it gently over both your and your partner's crotch before sex. Everyone thought the Pope opposed contraception because of rigid, centuries-old church doctrine; turns out he just likes things easy-peasy hippie style!

The Rock Doctor Is In

The Blind Boys of Alabama don't go anywhere without this man.

By Dr. Jon Wurster, Specialist in Entertainment Medicine

My name is Dr. Jon Wurster, M.D., and my specialty is entertainment medicine. For twenty-five years I've traveled the globe, bringing my healing touch to many of the music world's biggest stars.

Some backstory: In the summer of 1985, about a year out of medical school, I was manning the graveyard shift at Raleigh Community Hospital, in North Carolina. I'd just finished closing a stab wound when a nurse approached with a look of absolute horror. "Dr. Wurster," she said, "I think you'd better come to room 205 immediately." As I approached, I could hear a moaning so intense I wasn't sure if it was coming from a man or a dog. What I saw lying in the bed was approximately 23 years of age, writhing in sheer agony. It was a man.

Seconds later, I was pulled aside by a mustachioed bruiser wearing a satin jacket with the name Bobzilla stitched above the left breast. Bobzilla informed me that he was the tour manager for the heavy-metal band Keel, among other groups, and that the victim, Ricky, was the band's bassist. I was told there'd been an after-show mishap involving Ricky, a groupie, and a spent canister of Reddi-Wip. In order to heighten the sexual experience of being manually pleasured by the groupie, Ricky instructed a member of the band's road crew to place the open end of the canister into his anus just as he was about to climax. In theory, the canister would release a blast of CO_2 into the bassist's orifice, heightening his orgasm. Unfortunately, the roadie, who was under the influence of a crack-cocaine-and-amyl-nitrate cocktail, did not empty the canister's contents before placing the nozzle in Ricky's derriere. The result was . . . well, it was exactly what you're imagining, only much more horrific. Ricky also suffered severe abrasions on his penis from the 50-grit sandpaper he'd requested that the groupie use. It was messy, but I soon patched Ricky up and sent him and Bobzilla on their way.

I was surprised to receive a phone call from Bobzilla several weeks later, asking if I'd sign on as the physician for some rock tours. Seems my bedside manner, as well as my ability to keep the incident out of the papers, had impressed him, and before I knew it I'd become known as "the Rock Doctor."

Life on the road provided an eye-opening, often shocking education for a small-town country boy. I was quite taken aback by the sheer volume of sex-related illnesses and injuries I was treating, and I soon learned that these misfortunes did not discriminate due to age, gender, race, or style of music.

A short list of some of the more traditional problems I treated:

Urinary-tract infection (Scorpions, Vixen, Jesus Lizard, A Flock of Seagulls)

Genital crabs (Van Halen, Blind Boys of Alabama, A Flock of Seagulls, Wilco)

Gonorrhea (Decemberists, Cannibal Corpse, A Flock of Seagulls, Methods of Mayhem)

Herpes (normal and flagrant) (Kiss, A Flock of Seagulls, Tone Lōc, Interpol)

Hepatitis (10,000 Maniacs, Jet, A Flock of Seagulls)

Genital warts (Dokken, A Flock of Seagulls, Spoon)

But there was never a shortage of 3:00 a.m. calls to my hotel room from someone requesting urgent, 100 percent confidential medical attention. A few that come to mind:

Third-degree rope burns (Chicago's horn section)

Penis disentanglement (Allman Brothers, .38 Special)

Microphone extraction (anal) (GG Allin)

Microphone extraction (vaginal) (Courtney Love, A Flock of Seagulls, Courtney Love again)

My experiences gave me a fascinating glimpse into the mind of the rock star. They showed the lengths to which these people go to experience the pleasures of the flesh. My patients were ingenious when it came to facilitating their sexual escapades. When condoms or dental dams were unavailable, they'd improvise with whatever was handy, be it an umbrella sheath (Men at Work's Greg Ham) or the shrink-wrap on an LP (all of the Bangles). Why, I once came across one of the boys in the Ocean Blue (I could never keep them straight) having sex with a tub of Elmer's glue just before going onstage, because he needed to get his dick wet "right the fuck now, Doc." Guess who spent five hours trying to pry this kid's penis from his tighty whiteys?

Incidents like that often caused me to ask if I was putting my healing talents to their best use. Surely there were children in Third World countries who would benefit more from my gift than some drunken goon who broke his ankle jumping off a bed after winning the Monsters of Metal Masturbation contest (Iced Earth guitarist Randall Shawver), right? Yet somehow I couldn't walk away from it all. These artists were my family . . . or so I thought.

Perhaps you've noticed I haven't shied away from using the names of the performers I've traveled with and treated. There is a reason for this. Not one of them came to my defense when charges of extreme malpractice and medical perversion (among others) were levied against me last year. It seems that a double standard exists for the rock star and the lowly man on the street. Apparently you can have intercourse with members of three generations of one family in a single night (Kenny G) and nobody blinks an eye, but when a 17-year-old Weezer fan's acute state of inebriation requires a nude full-body rubdown to get blood flowing away from her fists and down toward her genitals, it's some kind of crime. I knew we'd end up in a goddamn police state if that Obama cat got elected.

Dr. Jon Wurster
Inmate 35828937488
Leavenworth, Kansas

READERS TALK:
HOW DO WE STAY SAFE?

Ben, age 42

I always use my condom, and I always make sure it's in working condition. That means washing it with soap and water inside and out and injecting it with fresh nonoxynol-9 every two weeks. If it rips, I stitch it up immediately. When it loses its sheen, I buff it with a special latex chamois. I just purchased a brace for the reservoir tip that looks like a hollowed-out button and that should reduce the chance of bursting by 35 to 40 percent, at least according to the "Shame Shame Shame" segment on Fox.

Holly, age 29

There's something called tannis root, which is actually more of a tuber than an actual root. You just steep it in boiling water and drink it like a tea. Honestly, it doesn't taste great—kind of like stale licorice—but it does supercharge your immune system, preventing sexually transmitted diseases from breaching your natural defenses. Furthermore, my vagina just caved in.

HEY, DIDJA KNOW...

An early form of birth control was having oneself struck by lightning?

Most instances of condom breakage can be blamed on large-scale, organized sperm heists?

So-called "double bagging" with condoms is never recommended, unless your penis is the size and weight of a gallon milk jug?

Blue balls, or "lover's nuts," can be best avoided by having your date place an ice pack on your groin and then leaving quickly so you can ride out the pain alone?

The earliest form of birth control ever recorded was the "Dead Sea mud plug"?

Most sexually transmitted diseases can be easily cured through time travel?

CHAPTER 8

SEXUAL DYSFUNCTION

COMMON PROBLEMS FACED

BY OTHER PEOPLE

"Sorry, I'm just not in the mood."

"I swear this never happens."

*"Have you ever seen The Serpent and the Rainbow? I ask because
it's as if my genitals are in this weird third realm between life and
death, like the zombies that supposedly exist in Haiti."*

**Not us, right? We're *different*.
Each and every time we make
love, our penis rises as solid
and immovable as a monolith,
and our vagina is as moist and**
pleasingly fragrant as a halved tangerine. Our orgasms are neither
awkwardly early nor bruisingly delayed, and we have no reason
to believe that our partner is spending the duration of intercourse
hoping a drunk driver rams his vehicle through our bedroom wall.

But *someone's* not enjoying sex. Sales of products designed to
treat sexual dysfunction—erection splints and ejaculation-inhibiting
pincers, libido implants and lubrication spritzers—have done nothing but increase, ever since colonial silversmiths first began making impotence goblets back in the early eighteenth century. Most of
these so-called cures, however, offer nothing but fleeting, bankrupt
hope. With the exception of the MachoMax line of Turgidity Shakes
and Stamina Snackers, the only real way to deal with sexual dysfunction is with the knowledge and understanding found within this
chapter.

Impotence and premature ejaculation are the two most common
erectile-dysfunction conditions in men. While frustrating, these
problems need not interfere with a vigorous sex life. For example,
some women dislike the sternness of the fully engorged erection,

preferring instead a gentler, semisoft organ that just lolls inside the vagina like a rag doll. Other women prize the premature ejaculator, affectionately known as the "express Casanova," for the alacrity he demonstrates in climaxing even before she has her bra unclasped.

In women, on the other hand, most dysfunction involves a problem in the sexual-response cycle—loss of libido, inability to reach orgasm, and so on. The source of these problems is often not obvious, so women are often left to juggle a variety of plausible possibilities. Anxiety or estrogen vampires? Diabetes or the fact her husband initiates lovemaking with "I'll be wearing not one, not two, but three blindfolds to ensure my eyes do not glimpse the atrocity of your aging body"?

Of course, as we said, it's never us. We have nothing to worry about. Everyone else, though, should probably keep reading.

THE 800-POUND GORILLA LYING INCAPACITATED IN THE CORNER OF THE ROOM:
DISCUSSING INTIMATE PROBLEMS WITH YOUR PARTNER

Still reading, huh? Not to worry. We were kidding before. Every one of us here at ABS has at one time or another suffered from what we affectionately refer to as "Droopsy's Revenge." What we're saying is that you're not alone.

It sure is easy to feel alone and awkward, though, when you're faced with a sexual dilemma in the bedroom—even if you're literally by yourself! (Solo sexual dysfunction is more common than you might think. To learn more, see Malcolm Jamal-Warner's 1994 medical thriller, *Daaaamn!*)

We here at ABS have found that the best way to start a dialogue about the tricky subject of sexual dysfunction is to actually treat it the same way you would an 800-pound gorilla lying limp in the corner of the room. Here are three suggested actions based on this metaphor:

1. Scream
2. Run from the room
3. Kill it

But first, let's find out what we're dealing with. Just how messed up are you? And what exactly can we do to help you about it? Read on . . .

QUIZ: HAVE YOU LOST YOUR ERECTION?

If left unaddressed, impotence can ruin a relationship. Adding to the frustration is the fact that the condition is easy to miss if you're not paying attention. While a doctor can inject your penis with a special radioactive dye, and scan it with sophisticated tumescence-detection equipment, the best you can do at home is to watch for the signs that any layperson can pick up on. The next time you're unsure if you've lost your erection, take the following short quiz.

1. Which fictional character best characterizes the state of your penis?
   a. Dr. Jekyll
   b. Mr. Hyde
   c. Mary, the retarded maidservant

2. Observe the silhouette of your penis against a lit wall. What are you looking at?
   a. A mighty javelin
   b. A fully loaded pistol
   c. A lit wall, pretty much

3. As you thrust, what is your partner telling you?

 a. "Ram that cock in me!"

 b. "Jam that cock in me!"

 c. "Ever so carefully, thread that cock into me!"

4. If you were offered some free Viagra right now, would you take it?

 a. Nah. Maybe when I'm much older.

 b. Sure, just for kicks.

 c. I don't like the sound of that "if."

5. Which element on the periodic table would you say your penis most resembles?

 a. Iron

 b. Platinum

 c. Magnesium, if that's the one that always makes women finish themselves off with a vibrator.

To determine your score, add up the number of times you selected (c).

 0 Oh, please.

 1–2 These things happen.

 3–4 You should probably talk to a doctor or anyone on the friendly staff of a Walmart drop-in clinic.

 5 No worries—you just have a vagina.

SEXUAL ARTS AND CRAFTS: THE GUILT QUILT

We all harbor guilt, especially in regards to sexual dysfunction. If you keep a Guilt Quilt under your bed, you can reach for it at any lull in the action and add a stitch or two. Who knows, the sight of Sunbonnet Sue might just get you in the mood again!

WHEN YOUR DONG WON'T DING, AND YOUR SLIT'S ON THE FRITZ:

A SERIOUS NOTE ABOUT IMPOTENCE AND FRIGIDITY

From time to time, all men and women experience some form of sexual impotence. Often, there is no medical explanation—or cure. Rather, most people believe impotence or frigidity is a product of anxiety, the natural aging process, or simply being a pathetic, limp-dicked sack-of-shit husband who wishes he were even one-fourth the man that Carl from accounting is. The point is, we don't really know what causes impotence, and most of us don't care, because we've moved on to someone younger who really "gets" us and has turned us on to a lot of really interesting things, like freeganism and emo music. So, hey, best of luck with your wiener worries!

This is the face of female frigidity . . .

. . . and this is her name and current mailing address.

MOST COMMON EXCUSES FOR IMPOTENCE

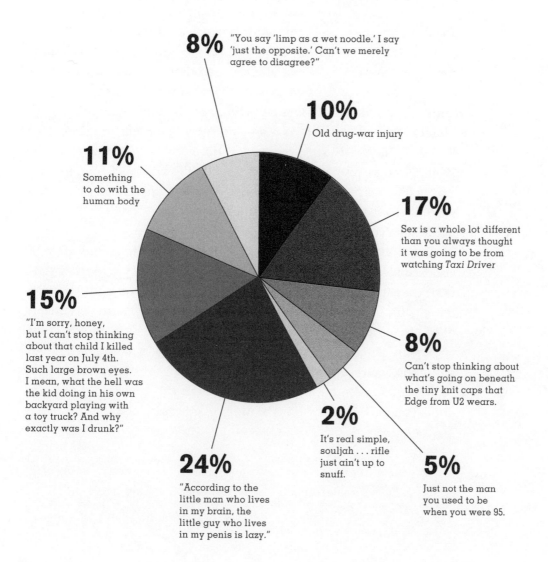

8% "You say 'limp as a wet noodle.' I say 'just the opposite.' Can't we merely agree to disagree?"

10% Old drug-war injury

11% Something to do with the human body

17% Sex is a whole lot different than you always thought it was going to be from watching *Taxi Driver*

15% "I'm sorry, honey, but I can't stop thinking about that child I killed last year on July 4th. Such large brown eyes. I mean, what the hell was the kid doing in his own backyard playing with a toy truck? And why exactly was I drunk?"

8% Can't stop thinking about what's going on beneath the tiny knit caps that Edge from U2 wears.

2% It's real simple, souljah . . . rifle just ain't up to snuff.

5% Just not the man you used to be when you were 95.

24% "According to the little man who lives in my brain, the little guy who lives in my penis is lazy."

I HAVE A HEADACHE FOR THE FORESEEABLE FUTURE: LOSS OF LIBIDO IN WOMEN

You'd love to have sex with your partner. And why wouldn't you? He's still the very same man with a steady job and tolerable criminal record you settled for when you realized time was quickly running out and you had to take whatever was most convenient within your building complex. But there he is lying on the other side of the bed, glumly looking down at his naked body and past his flagging erection at a *Kitchen Nightmares* rerun. His hopes for the evening are fading, and so are yours. All that's left is the half-mumbled excuse that you're not feeling well, or work is stressing you out. Or maybe you just wordlessly cover yourself in leaves and hope that your partner forgets you're even in the room.

Some women, for reasons even they don't often understand, suddenly find themselves greeting intercourse with the indifference of a spoiled princess having her nether region sprayed with a fancy fragrance. Or, worse, they become openly hostile or fearful of the act, increasingly referring to their partner's penis as "that spongy, poisonous wand." While the most obvious step is to consult your doctor or to visit a museum of natural history in search of helpful sarcophagus inscriptions, there are several other measures you and your partner should immediately look into.

Relaxation

Women usually need more time to ease into lovemaking than men, so there's no need to rush. Look for nonsexual ways to unwind. You can prepare yourself by taking a soothing bubble bath or "chilling out" for three months in an opium den.

Distraction

Many women become so preoccupied with their bodies during intercourse that they actually undermine themselves. So give your mind something else to do. Women in our studies have found that singing a peppy song—ideally into an amplified device—is a terrific way to avoid unhealthy self-monitoring, and get those magnificent endorphins surging. By the time they've finished "Old Man River" for the third time, their partner has ejaculated and the entire grueling affair is over.

Stimulation

While some women battle sexual anxiety, others simply have difficulty getting revved up. In a less hectic era, a woman could spend time with an erotic novel and use her imagination to prime her libido. With our modern-day schedules, however, this is an impractical if not impossible task. Fortunately, with stimulatory aids such as the ABS line of erotic trifold pamphlets, you can receive all the masturbatory escapism you require in a hundred words. Here is one of our best-selling titles, Rogue of Thighs, *in its entirety:*

It was just November, but winter had arrived early at Heathmoor. Although the snow had shrouded the paths of the estate, Genevieve knew her way by heart—she was, wouldn't you know, all of 19 and beautiful, and had roamed these grounds since she was but a wee child. She stopped upon noticing horse tracks. These looked familiar. Perhaps the beast carried her manservant, Rimshot? It had been two weeks since she had taken every blood-engorged inch of his buccaneer's purple-tipped spear into her dewy quiver-purse. This was just after she had nursed a wounded dragon back to health with homemade cookies and hours-long exotic rubdowns.

Note: Technically, this story runs 106 words, but no cuts could have been made without sacrificing the beauty of the tale.

WHEN BITS DON'T FIT:
IMPROVING SEXUAL COMPATIBILITY THROUGH INVASIVE AND POTENTIALLY LIFE-THREATENING SURGICAL PROCEDURES

Imagine this scenario: You and your partner have enjoyed a healthy courtship—flirting, light petting, sharing a bidet—and have finally agreed to consummate your relationship. With the ink still fresh on your signed and notarized Consent to Perform Intercourse Form (CS-1019.c, available at the public library), your engorged genitals meet for the first time and—*access denied.* Maybe he suffers from a fussy cubic shaft, or she is afflicted with labyrinthine vaginal disorder. Whatever the case, the bits simply don't fit.

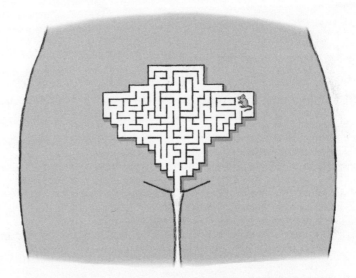

The medical condition known as labyrinthine vaginal disorder can be overcome through costly surgeries or a brief consultation with an editor at *Games* magazine.

Luckily, where our own bodies fail us, science finds a way. There are a number of cosmetic procedures gaining popularity in the field of genital reimagineering, particularly in countries unburdened by nitpicky medical-malpractice laws. These procedures are still highly experimental and come with a substantial danger of disfigurement or even death but, honestly, who among us hasn't risked far worse for one to two minutes of sexual gratification?

PENIS WHITTLING

For the unfortunate male cursed with a thick, trunk-like penis, finding a mate with an accommodating (i.e., yawning, cavernous) vagina can prove challenging. However, through a process known as penis whittling, the penis can undergo a therapy of chemical peels. Over time, this treatment can shave off up to one inch of circumference while also providing the shaft with a smooth, glassy surface.

Risk factor: Medium.
An unevenly applied peel can result in a penis with an unattractive hourglass shape (or a stunning lozenge shape).

CONSENSUAL TWIZZLING

For years, the only remedy for plumping one's narrow, reed-like penis was to insert it into a wasps' nest and hope for the best. These days, you and your partner can elect to be surgically "twizzled." With this procedure, both partners' genitals are implanted with subdermal grooves, like a perfectly interlocking nut and screw.

Risk factor: High.
While still an improvement over clumsy cock anchors, the highly customized nature of twizzling guarantees you one partner for life. But aggressive thrusting can also cause stripping. A majority of physicians recommend inserting the penis slowly—in a smooth, clockwise motion—to prevent such a disaster.

CONSENSUAL TWIZZLING

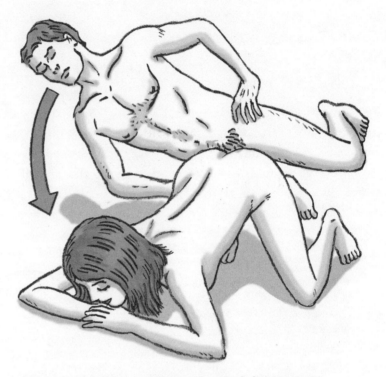

To insert and withdraw one's penis, the twizzled partner must
remember one simple rule: righty-tighty, lefty-loosey.

THE TRUE VALUE™ GENITAL MORTISE HINGE

Perfected by the excellent people at True Value Hardware ("Start
Right, Start Here"), this process involves the penis and reattaching
these segments with a series of opposing bronze hinges. The procedure allows the penis to successfully navigate even the most mad-
dening vaginal maze.

Risk factor: Variable.

Risk is minimal if one regularly applies food-grade machine
lubricant to the hinges. (We recommend the True Value brand, Deli
Flavor Saver.) However, without proper upkeep there is a significant
danger of genital oxidation.

LABIAL PROSTHETIC INSERTS

A corrective solution to the classic square-peg/round-hole problems associated with incompatibly shaped genitals. These swappable disks—inspired by a pastry chef's icing-extrusion gun—can modify the vaginal opening to welcome even the most oddly shaped penises.

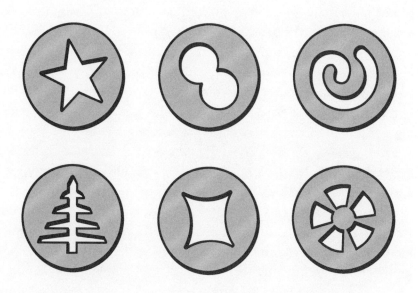

These labial inserts can accommodate most common penis shapes.

Risk factor: Low.

Remember to store your labial inserts in a cool, dry place, and be sure to keep them away from Mother around the holidays!

PREMATURE EJACULATION:
THE UNKINDEST SQUIRT

William Masters and Virginia Johnson were a team of sex researchers who also happened to be married to each other. (Um, gimmicky,
ya think?) Though most of their achievements pale in comparison to
what ABS will one day accomplish, just as soon as the Department
of Health and Human Services gets off our backs, Masters and Johnson at least deserve *some* credit for their efforts in conquering that
familiar scourge of masculine sexuality: premature ejaculation.

Premature ejaculation—or "birthing a preemie"—could mean the
typical scenario of a man experiencing an orgasm in his pants during heavy petting, but it could also refer to any instance of ejaculation that is ill-timed or inconvenient to the community at large (during a national moment of silence, for instance, or when it's your turn
to exit the space shuttle). Basically, whenever your penis pulls a real
boner (figuratively speaking, as the penis should *never* be punished
for literal boners), it most likely counts as premature ejaculation.

But back to our old friends Masters and Johnson. Their break-
through technique for overcoming premature ejaculation requires
months of dedicated practice, and the full participation of both partners before it yields any results. We at ABS just knew we could do
better, and we think you'll find that our prolonging techniques beat
Masters and Johnson in every respect.

SIX (UPDATED) TRICKS TO SLOW EJACULATION

We all wish we could hold on to the ecstasy of coitus for a few precious moments longer, before the inevitably lovely *la petite mort* and accompanying corrosive burn of ejaculate fluid. And maybe we can.

While none of these techniques for avoiding premature ejaculation is 100% guaranteed, all of them vastly improve upon methods suggested in previous printings of this book. (See *Our Bodies, Our Junk* first edition, page 155, "The Casanova's Secret Weapon: Urethral Searing.")

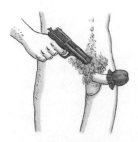

RENDITION

Often, ejaculation can be slowed by frightening the penis with the threat of torture in a foreign country that does not adhere to the protocols of the Geneva Convention.

VISUAL MISDIRECTION

A troubling, well-placed printed message can distract the penis.

GUILT

Invite a family victimized by current downward economic trends to watch you make love. Guilty feelings about their plight, contrasted with your obvious good fortune, could delay your orgasm by a full minute.

VARIABLE TEMPERATURE

Subject the penis to alternating extreme temperatures. This technique has proven extremely effective by the U.S. armed forces.

RECONNECT WITH HIGH SCHOOL FRIENDS

Take a breather by spending a few moments updating your Facebook status.

UNWELCOME FRICTION

Immerse your penis in wet paste, then roll it in loose gravel and wait 15–20 minutes until it's dry to the touch. This gravel glaze will produce just enough friction to prolong lovemaking indefinitely, or until one or both of you can no longer bear the pain.

OUR BENEFACTOR, MACHOMAX

The operating costs of a cutting-edge sex-research organization like ABS can be staggering, particularly when certain federal agencies refuse grant money to fund studies that may end in weeping or internal-genital bruising. (As if they can't trust subjects to read the fine print on a release form. Ever heard of a nanny state? Well, you're living in one, pal.) To make ends meet we have occasionally sought funding from nontraditional sources, most notably our good friends at Honduras-based herbal supplement manufacturer MachoMax. Allow us to tell you a bit about MachoMax, so you can see for yourself just how off-base ABC's John Stossel has been about them.

True, MachoMax began life as the funding arm of a Tegucigalpa-based paramilitary organization. But the militia's name, which translates to "Men in Hoods Whose Mouths Drip Blood," is perhaps misleading. Our MachoMax contact, Benito, has assured us that the group's responsibilities mostly involve culling goats after livestock epidemics. Allow Benito to tell you about MachoMax's humble origins:

> After the infected "goats" are exterminated and the other, more obedient "goats" of the village are taught to think twice before exposing themselves to such a terrible, terrible disease, the men waste time carousing and abusing the potent mixture of heroin and gunpowder called "brown brown." But our leader is a very brilliant man with many ideas for business, who is quite capable of making love to dozens of women in a row and impregnating them all. One morning, tightening the sash around his imported Italian bathrobe, he wondered, "What if we could sell my sexual prowess in small foil packets for large prices at the gas-station counters of the great country America?"

The revered leader of MachoMax

Inspiring, no? Though we have yet to speak directly to this prodigiously talented leader—from what we understand, he is an elusive presence even at MachoMax headquarters, and is known to most of his men only as a shadowy entity who appears to them at night and pins down their chest and furiously tickles their armpits—we certainly admire his enterprising spirit. Since the company's founding, MachoMax has rolled out roughly 480 sexual enhancement supplements, many of which contain the active ingredient bone meal, and, despite the public's negative perception of unregulated substances, are essentially no more dangerous than, say, a gummy bear dusted in trace amounts of rat dander.

Our contract with MachoMax stipulates that ABS provide endorsements for a number of supplements treating various forms of sexual dysfunction. We do so with the hope that you will consume these products wisely—say, in minuscule doses, mixed in an extremely weak 50:1 water/supplement solution—and with the understanding that we are either deeply excited or deeply sorry about whatever comes next.

MACHOMAX ENDORSEMENTS

Product: **Circus Pole Erection Powder**

The MachoMax promise:
Long, girthy erections, "like the strongest pole in the big top."

ABS endorsement:
The mild hallucinations induced by Circus Pole are indeed carnivalesque.

Product: **"¡Ay Papí Grande!" Sex Cry Amplifier**

The MachoMax promise:
"Increase the volume and duration of her love cries for your thrust."

ABS endorsement:
Works as advertised, possibly due to the burning sensation reported in the subject's voice box.

Product: **Caste of Kings Glans Whitener**

The MachoMax promise:
"She will salivate for your high-status white rod."

ABS endorsement:
Apparently some Central and South American countries place a social premium on lighter skin shades. The product does indeed have a noticeable bleaching effect, but should last, at most, only fifteen to twenty years.

Product: **Raul Julia's Choice Ejaculate Propulsion Powder**

The MachoMax promise:
"Shoot it across the room like Raul Julia himself!"

ABS endorsement:
We're sure the estate of the late, great Raul Julia would object to his likeness being used in this manner. Apparently laws are different in Honduras. Causes dry heaves, but no significant vomiting.

Product: **Yerba Maté Vaginal Lubricating Powder**

The MachoMax promise:
"Makes panties slick with the enchanting taste of yerba."

ABS endorsement:
This supplement is relaxing when steeped in hot water or gin.

Product: **Amazon Cock Prince Penis Enlargener**

The MachoMax promise:
"Largest cock in your neighborhood. Period."

ABS endorsement:
From what we can tell, this is just a chicken-mole tamale, though not an unflavorful one. Try it with a dab of sour cream or Greek yogurt.

Product: **Adiós El Madre Catholic Sex Powder**

The MachoMax promise:
"Makes the dirtiest sex invisible to the Virgin Mary."

ABS endorsement:
True to the guarantee on the packaging. Since using, we have not experienced "the anger of the saints," but it has caused heart explosion in a small number of collegiate test subjects.

NO ONE'S PERFECT, ESPECIALLY NOT US

Over the years, we here at the Association for the Betterment of Sex have had quite a few successes in regard to scientific studies and trials. To name just three:

- In 2005, we confirmed that the vast majority of adolescents are not huge fans when it comes to participating in "hugging sessions" with sex researchers who haven't been properly introduced.

- In 2007, we found that all a man really has to do to impress a lady is to extend a pinky finger when placing on a condom. This will signal class. A posh New England accent, or what passes for one these days, can also help tremendously.

- In 2010, we learned that just by spraying a hint of Jordan, Michael Jordan's cologne spray for men, on your rear end, your chances of ending up with the wrong type of woman increase from around 50 percent to 95 percent. We couldn't believe it, either.

But as with any group specializing in sex that operates out of an office with no official lab or bathroom, ABS has also had its share of scientific failures. Are we embarrassed by this? Sure. Will this somehow prevent us from spreading the word about our failures? No way! Publicity is publicity.

Here are the top eleven ABS studies that didn't turn out quite as planned, in order of severity of injury or loss of life:

1. "Can Condoms Break in Space? How About on a Carnival Ride?"

2. "Oral Contraceptives, Testosterone, and Sexuality in Regard to Steve Doocy of *FOX & Friends*"

3. "Milk, Milk, Lemonade, Where Exactly Is Fudge Made?"

4. "Understanding Risky and Compulsive Sex Behavior in Bald Eagles and Other Nearly Extinct Animals"

5. "Johnny King, the One and Only Cult Leader in the World Who Never Gets Laid: What's Up with That Guy?"

6. "Testicles Are Just Plain Goofy-Lookin', Ain't They?"

7. "Horrific Airplane Crashes and How They Affect Erection Loss"

8. "How Much Pubic Lice Is Too Much Pubic Lice?"

9. "A Group of Homeless Men Standing Around a Burn Barrel: How Long Before the Kissin' and Huggin' Begins?"

10. "Keepin' the Needle a-Peakin' and the Chicks a-Squeakin': Talking Dirty with '70s CB Slang"

11. "Senior Citizens: Well? Still got *it*?"

HEY, DIDJA KNOW...

Worldwide, there are approximately 320 acts of sexual intercourse each day?

In 1976, men successfully negotiated the cutoff point for premature ejaculation down from 3 minutes 17 seconds to 2 minutes 33 seconds?

Twenty percent of women can only achieve orgasm while watching figure skating on a large-screen plasma television?

Bologna is a tremendous aphrodisiac, but only when placed directly onto the genitals and aggressively taste-tested?

The first president, George Washington, had a thing for Vietnamese chicks?

Houdini had more than 50,000 lovers, all pretty ugly?

If you bump and grind, your lover's gonna lose their mind. But if you cower and shake, your lover is gonna leave to bake a cake? (source: Confucius)

Nearly 25 percent of women have, at one time or another, faked experiencing a fake orgasm?

A man's penis will regenerate like the tail of a lizard if pulled off? But only in a hot, dry climate, like Dubai?

CHAPTER 9

HOMOSEXUALITY

THE OTHER

STRAIGHT

When the gentleman who came to fix our photocopier asked if he could use our phone (because he left his "out in the truck"), we didn't even blink.

Although we declined what was an obvious invitation for homosexual group sex, we accepted—nay, we silently *honored*—his lifestyle choice to love other men. So what if he mistook us all for homosexuals? When a male cashier once asked a member of ABS if he should put the receipt in the plastic bag, our colleague didn't recoil in disgust at this clear request for intercourse in a curtained booth in the sub-basement of a dance club called the Lancelot. He merely smiled at the cashier and said, "I'm flattered, but no thanks. I've got a cousin you might like, though."

But, sadly, in much of this country, to be gay is to be despised. For instance, most states have laws prohibiting gay marriage. Also, gays still can't serve in the military, and the word "queer" was unceremoniously removed from the dime in the early 1980s. It seems nothing brings out hostility in our culture like homosexuality, and, unfortunately, it doesn't look like we're going to change anyone's mind in the near future.

All we at ABS can do is *educate*. In the past, we've had consultants lead tribadism clinics open to the community at large, but it's our hope that this book can affect an even wider audience with our inclusive message. If millions of heterosexuals like you can trust us for tips on finding the G-spot while scuba diving or while waiting for the dilation eye drops to work at the ophthalmologist's office, surely you can trust us as we present the following primer in the same-sex arts.

ARE YOU IN THE PRESENCE OF A HOMOSEXUAL?

Homosexuality is a recent phenomenon, right up there with scrapbooking and flashing gang signs while posing for wedding photos. In fact, homosexuality is such a newfangled conceit that we are hard-pressed to come up with any distinguishing characteristics for it. It would be real easy for us to merely claim, "Watch Robin Williams in *The Birdcage,* or Tom Cruise in his latest Scientology video." But to look at a complete stranger, and within five to ten seconds determine if that person is indeed a homosexual takes a special skill. And it's a skill that all of us at ABS have managed to teach ourselves while spending an awful lot of time at karaoke joints located near military bases.

Just by a mere glance or a quick peek through our fingers we have developed the ability to pick up on various homosexual "tells," or distinguishing clues that give away one's sexuality. What follows are a few. But we should warn you that there are many, many exceptions to these rules. And, just to make life even more difficult, homosexuals will often give out false tells just to fool others. Homosexuals, like the rest of us, can be a wily bunch!

- Big toe same size as middle finger
- Nostrils flare when talking about Bette Midler
- Sign of the beast somewhere on upper torso
- Chain on wallet is longer than rat tail
- Knows all the lyrics to Ace of Base songs
- Hands tremble when given a compliment about muscle mass

- At ease in cowboy hats, even when the chin strap is used
- Birkenstocks smell like wasabi peas
- Exhibits a forceful, aggressive, or loud demeanor when hair is mussed
- Seems pleasant enough, even when directly asked if they are "a gay"
- Once slept with Ronnie James Dio
- Not shy about high-fiving amusement-park mascots

THE DA VINCI CODE, BUT GAYER: DECRYPTING THE SECRET GAY LANGUAGE OF PUBLIC-RESTROOM STALLS

It's no secret that since America's founding, homosexual men have employed a coded language to help cope with the occasional difficulties of their alternative lifestyle.

This language often appears in the form of pictograms etched on bathroom stalls of public restrooms from coast to coast. This is sometimes a warning, sometimes instructions, and, at other times, just a way of broadcasting one's desire to perform a reach-around on strangers after they complete their bowel movement.

 "Someone took a two-flusher in here recently. Ergo, this stall is less than ideal for gay sex with a stranger."

 "Warning: there is a good chance of running into your dad in this stall."

 "I will fellate you, no questions asked—as long as you're okay with the fact that I kind of resemble the Monopoly guy."

 "Just looking to hug and talk for a little while."

 "I have an extra-long penis, and I like to stand naked before my large porthole window."

 "It's cozy in here." (Can also mean "Looking to have sex with someone approximately my own height.")

 "Attention toilet users: did anyone ever find my wedding band?"

 "Have you seen the latest Batman film? It was really good, and this is coming from someone who usually doesn't go for all those comic-book movies. You know what I mean?"

 "For the life of me, I can't remember any of the words to 'Karma Chameleon.'"

THIRTY-ONE FLAVORS OF GAY:
THIS YEAR'S ROSTER

We now know that the assumption that there exists only two varieties of homosexual—campy and kitschy—is well off the mark. How do we know this? We've studied other peoples' research.

There are, it seems, as many varieties of gay as there are yummy colors in a colorful set of rainbow magic markers. This begs the question: Which color are you?

MALE

TYPE: TWINK

Physical appearance:
Thin, pale to the point of translucence; hairless; mottled with hickies.

Dress:
Nude, except for a bow tie and dog tags.

Preferred meeting place:
Bus stations; after shift at American Apparel; high in the forest canopy.

Drink/food of choice:
Red Bull; Twizzlers.

Turn-ons:
Webcams; Lukas Haas.

Turnoffs:
Guys who don't bruise on contact.

Typical small talk:
"OMG, I knew Sasha back when we used to go-go dance in Oslo!"

TYPE: BEAR

Physical appearance:

Husky and hairy; Paul Bunyan meets Chewbacca.

Dress:

Cuffed denim; flannel; scoop-neck football jerseys.

Preferred meeting place:

Bars or churches with "Rough" or "Raw" in the name.

Drink/food of choice:

Domestic beer; raw sirloin.

Turn-ons:

Beards; river salmon.

Turnoffs:

Linen slacks.

Typical small talk:

"Goddamn it! Anyone know how to get saltwater taffy out of back hair?"

TYPE: LEATHER DADDY

Physical appearance:

Butch; musclebound; close-cropped hair.

Dress:

Clad all in leather (boots, biker cap, vest for retail job at Staples).

Preferred meeting place:

Bars called "Thor's Hammer"; public dungeons; Judas Priest videos.

Drink/food of choice:

Vodka and lemon-lime Slice.

Turn-ons:

The feel of the whip (be it the handle or the lash).

Turnoffs:

Merlot; rancid lube; the staunch heterosexuality of Motörhead's Lemmy.

Typical small talk:

"Jude Law was truly wonderful as that robot prostitute in *A.I.*"

TYPE: INSUFFERABLE OLD QUEEN

Physical appearance:

Flabby; balding; pasty; occasional Kaposi's sarcoma.

Dress:

Scarves; sandals; kimonos with plenty of roomy pockets for "poppers."

Preferred meeting place:

Lounges with tons of throw pillows, scattered about just so.

Drink/food of choice:

Gin fizz; semen.

Turn-ons:

Twinks; parades.

Turnoffs:

Performance fleece.

Typical small talk:

"If you're staying, I'm paying. But if you're going, I'm a-ho-ing."

TYPE: CLOSETED HOMOSEXUAL

Physical appearance:

Unassuming; occasional regretful erection.

Dress:

Button-down shirt; khakis with dark spot of pre-ejaculate.

Preferred meeting place:

Rest stops; airport bathrooms; rented cars.

Drink/food of choice:

Non-alcoholic beer; Arby's.

Turn-ons:

Secrets; twinks.

Turnoffs:

PTA meetings; undercover policemen.

Typical small talk:

"This never happened."

FEMALE

TYPE: BULL DYKE

Physical appearance:

Little fireplug with a whole lotta heart.

Dress:

Brawny paper-towels mascot, but with Tevas and chain wallet.

Preferred meeting place:

Food co-ops; YMCA.

Drink/food of choice:

Oolong tea; vegan beef jerky.

Turn-ons:

Native American crafts; getting a haircut at home.

Turnoffs:

A sense of humor.

Typical small talk:

"This nut loaf doesn't contain whey, does it?"

NOTE: Guys, the woman from the Rite Aid photo lab called and they lost the bull-dyke negatives. Can we reshoot with that locksmith lady?

TYPE: GARDEN-VARIETY LESBIAN

Physical appearance:

Pierced; tattooed; smells nice; seemingly engineered for lust.

Dress:

Confoundingly incomplete.

Preferred meeting place:

Lesbian bars; Wiccan shops.

Drink/food of choice:

Tequila; Sour Patch kids.

Turn-ons:

Abusive men; nurturing women; sight of own blood.

Turnoffs:

Memories of childhood.

Typical small talk:

"You're so good to me, and yet I've got to go. I'll send you a friend request!"

KNOW YOUR GAY SUBCULTURES: MALE

Chubbies

Description: Overweight or obese men

Turf: Your lap (especially if they want to bite your "meatball sub")

Special customs: Moving from safe house to safe house; in constant fear of "chubby chasers"

Initiation ritual: Developing bedsores

Two-Spirits

Description: Native Americans fulfilling opposite or multiple-gender roles

Turf: Feather boutiques; your trendier corn mazes

Special customs: Native Americans aren't big on custom

Initiation ritual: Like *A Man Called Horse*, but splashier

Solo Jocks

Description: Homosexual athletes, often operating on the down-low

Turf: Anywhere there is turf (real or Astro-)

Special customs: Mutual masturbation on an Olympic dais

Initiation ritual: An orgy, with Al Pacino's *Cruising* playing in the background

Scooterboys

Description: Gay skinheads

Turf: Hang out mostly on lists of improbable gay subcultures; might not survive outside a test tube

Special customs: High-pitched, flutey giggling punctuated with a head-butt

Initiation ritual: None. In fact, it's the only gay subculture that offers recruiting gifts (typically an iPod Shuffle)

Drag Queens

Description: Men who put elaborate effort into dressing and behaving like women

Turf: Mid-1990s independent films; the ten or so feet of "strutting space" in front of your uncle's vanity mirror

Special customs: Hogging karaoke mics

Initiation ritual: Good old-fashioned game of mumblety-peg

KNOW YOUR GAY SUBCULTURES: FEMALE

Lipstick Lesbians

Description: Effeminate lesbians who often dress fashionably

Turf: Lipstick lesbians typically live alone, often in a big, spooky house on a hill

Special customs: Applying lipstick, doing that thing with the lips to spread the lipstick, daubing at lipstick

Initiation ritual: Must carry on a tumultuous relationship with the wife of former husband

Drag Kings

Description: Women who put elaborate effort into dressing and behaving like men

Turf: The fantastical Drag Kingdom

Special customs: Swaggering; taking just enough hormones to get a good John Waters 'stache going

Initiation ritual: Choreographed performance of the greaser half of "Summer Nights"

Granola Lesbians

Description: Earthy, eco-conscious lesbians

Turf: Anywhere there are bulk bins

Special customs: Adopting handicapped animals and parading them around, all holier-than-thou

Initiation ritual: Russian roulette

Bitches and Ho's Lesbians

Description: Lesbians, often Hispanic or black, influenced by gangsta-rap culture

Turf: Underground cave system in the Pakistani border town of Rawalpindi

Special customs: Scissoring in a way that intimidates white people

Initiation ritual: Very subdued: some candles, a Rudyard Kipling poem, and anything can happen

A FEW NEW GAY ROLE-PLAYING SCENARIOS

DEVELOPED BY ABS

FOR THE MALE

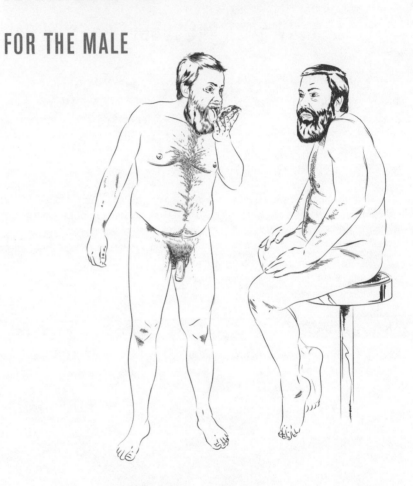

"THE OPEN-FACE REUBEN"
Closeted Indiana truck-stop
cook spots a "fellow traveler"
by the pie case. A furtive
lick of the stranger's kraut-
smothered Reuben is as close
as either man will ever come
to shared physical intimacy.

"OL' SAWBONES HAS A LOOK-SEE"

Your family physician always did have a certain twinkle in his eye when you showed up for your yearly football physical. Now that you're all grown up, it's time to reap the benefits of that finely aged passion.

"TURKEY TROT THROUGH THE CASTRO"

Somebody overindulged at last night's LGBT "Pornucopia" Thanksgiving banquet/Beth Ditto DJ set at Traxxx! Work off that turkey weight, boys! Note: For lesbians, this position is known as Stickin' & Lickin' the Landing.

FOR THE FEMALE

**"SHOPPING FOR SEITAN
AT THE PARK SLOPE CO-OP"**
Do they have that hard-to-find
brand you both enjoy? One
thing's for sure: finding out's
gonna be *fun!*

**"WE'RE THE HOTTEST
LESBIAN COUPLE ON
THIS *SEX AND THE CITY*
BUS TOUR"**
That bump in the road was
only Mario Cantone. Now just
lean back and enjoy this ride!

THE ABS GUIDE TO GAY PEACOCKING:

A WHOLE DIFFERENT ANIMAL

A peacock's plumes tend to come in many different and exotic colors. In about 2 percent of instances, however, the colors exactly mirror those of the Tennessee state flag.

Remember when we told you about peacocks being pompous and dirty little monsters, prone to showing off in order to divert attention from more-deserving animals, such as donkeys, mongooses, and humans? It's true. Peacocks are a plumed and feathery evolutionary disaster.

However, these ignorant fiends *do* have two good things going for them. One, they are very proficient at visiting hospitals and making the terminally ill laugh because of their innate ridiculousness. And two, they can teach us—*all* of us, no matter our sexual predilection—that it is quite possible to have sexual intercourse with a stranger regardless of how ugly we happen to be. This is a wonderful thing, and it's especially exciting for the homosexual male, who for years and years was told that good looks alone was the key ingredient to bedding another male.

This couldn't be further from the truth! What's *far* more important than appearance is a little something called *attitude*, especially if that attitude is really handsome and clothed in eccentric garments, the more bizarre and eye-catching the better. Yes, you're ugly and not very well liked by your co-workers or, for that matter, by your Lord. Does this mean that you're not worthy of getting laid just like more-attractive people? And if the answer is yes, can't you at least *try* to do something about your pathetic situation?

Again, peacocking is really not so difficult. Here is our foolproof method of attracting potential lovers of the *same* sex.*

---

*We are only talking about male homosexuals here. We aren't going to even begin to talk about lesbian peacocking. If that's your bag, check out the referees who work for the WNBA.

PEACOCKIN' THE GAY OL' WAY

1. Straw hats (perfect for, among other things, strawberry picking) are a must. You might also want to wear a T-shirt that reads GARDENERS GET SWEATY WHEN FORKING IN THEIR BEDS, but a half-shirt from Wake Forest University will work in a pinch.

2. Holding a tomato sandwich is gay code for "I am a conservative straight man who is only at this bar for the free food and the anal sex in the bathroom stalls."

3. Hearing aids (not visible) are a wonderful accessory. There is nothing wrong with having strangers feel sorry for you because you are deaf. Try also holding a large nineteenth-century ear trumpet to your head, or pretending that you are blind, crippled, and brain-dead. That can't hurt, either.

That's it. Luckily, gay men are infamous for not being too choosy or particular.

Gorillas in the Mist: Navigating the Sexual Dynamics of a Health-Club Steam Room

Since we thought it would be beneficial to report on this phenomenon firsthand, we sent Ted Travelstead, our Chief of Field-Studies Initiative officer, to a boutique men's health club and asked him to keep a journal of his experiences.

The researcher, before the bloom of innocence faded

March 4

Sitting in the locker room at the Bold Club. I'm fully clothed, gym bag at my feet, but already I get a sense that I'm being observed just as much as I'm observing. In the distance, I see the door to the steam room open, releasing a huge billowy cloud of white. What secrets lay inside that primordial mist? I'll soon find out. I bend and begin unlacing my boot . . .

March 6

Yesterday I entered the steam. With only a towel in my hand, I braced myself for the unknown as I let the searing mist engulf me. I could only make out huge hulking shapes at various spots throughout the large space. I chose a spot near the door and sat down. The hot tile stung my bare bottom. I waited. Loud grunts emanated from the mist, then a gasp. Nothing happened.

March 7

Today, contact. I moved camp farther from the door. I knew it was risky, as it would become more difficult to find my way out should something go wrong—and yet it was a chance I had to take. I sat for an hour, until every one of my pores was open like an infant's wailing mouth. My breathing became labored. I knew I couldn't stand this for much longer. Then it happened. From the dense haze, a shape began to materialize. His footsteps thundered beneath him as he approached, and as the distance between us closed I started to see him in detail. He was a massive, beautiful beast, muscles rippling, with large drops of moisture clinging to his moustache and man-turf below. His penis swung in a lazy arc between each knee like a giant flesh pendulum, producing a meaty thud upon contact with each side. Briefly, our eyes locked. He seemed to look into my very being as his hand brushed my knee in passing. Never have I felt so naked, so vulnerable. Then he was gone.

March 9

After a brief bout of respiratory distress, I'm back. I've decided that the subject I encountered the other day (from here on out I'll refer to him as "Phillip") must be the alpha of the group. Undoubtedly, he ventured forth to find out more about me. I hope I did my best to prove I come in peace. I think I must have passed some test, because I feel a certain openness here that didn't seem present before. While I didn't see Phillip today, I did encounter two younger males openly romping close by. Aware of my presence but not seeming to care, they shrieked and wrestled with reckless abandon, at one point even reaching out in tandem to slap my exposed buttocks as I bent to pick up my towel. Progress.

March 12

While I certainly haven't been accepted as one of their group, I am openly tolerated and have even been able to engage in the exploratory "sex play" afforded some of the more trusted outsiders. Yesterday, Phillip and another alpha I call "Craig" took me to a back corner filled with heavy steam and tossed me gently around like a sock puppet. It was an overwhelming experience, and while I never felt in any great danger it made me once again realize the great power these "people of the mist" are capable of. I suppose it doesn't hurt that there are gigantic racks of muscle-building weights only steps from here. The question remains: Is this steam-filled chamber the sacristy of their muscle church, or is it just the opposite? The questions, the mysteries!

March 15

I'm devastated to report that I had to suspend my field studies indefinitely due to a serious health problem. It seems that heavy exposure to the heat and humidity have caused the soles of my feet to slide off like the skins of two blanched tomatoes. Walking is torture, and to enter the steam in a wheelchair, or any other contraption, would mean almost certain exile. It may be a year before I can walk again, but when that time comes, I hope to again enter the unknown in order to find answers to the remaining questions about this fascinating species and their way of life. I can only pray they'll remember me when I return, for each and every one of their faces is etched inside my misty, broken heart.

HEY, DIDJA KNOW . . .

Forty percent of NRA members wistfully listen to Erasure under the blankets late at night?

Two-thirds of gays and lesbians had their first same-sex experience in a bumper car?

The height of the average glory hole has risen five inches, in proportion to the height increase in the average male since the early eighteenth century?

Most lesbians have never been parasailing?

Fonzie was the first openly gay character on television?

Testicles (also known as "tailor's plums") used to give off a pungent maple smell when engorged?

There has never been a gay puppeteer?

Fifty-seven percent of all homosexuals came out during "Day by Day" while watching a production of *Godspell*?

Despite popular wisdom, you can't simply "turn" gay? First you have to be bitten by a homosexual during a waxing moon.

Bisexuality is just a hoax perpetrated by the lip-gloss industry?

CONCLUSION

This book began with a less-than-modest proposal: a "radical new understanding of sex and intimacy." It is our hope that you now fully comprehend

what we meant by that statement—namely, that if you were to add every grain of sand in the world to the number of stars in the sky to the number of bees funneled onto Nicolas Cage's face in *The Wicker Man*, you still wouldn't even come close to approaching the sexual possibilities you now have at your disposal. That is, if you're reasonably attractive. If you're not, just stick to the masturbation chapter and try not to spill your lonesome, salty tears all over it.

So, what now? For one thing, you're probably wondering if it would actually be possible to meet us in person to thank us for the guidance you've received. The answer is yes, day or night, weeknight or holiday, whenever is most convenient for you. *Warning:* When visiting ABS headquarters, don't mention the fact that all five of us share a single desk, or that the receptionist appears to be nothing more than a Cyclops drawn onto the back of a Velcro dartboard. *Do* mention whether you're lactating, because we'd very much like to be involved in that somehow.

Are we available for round-the-clock house calls? Or to host Autoerotic Casino Night at your corporate gathering or VA hospital function? Or to sneak a few beefcake photos into your halfway house with the strict women-only policy? The answers are yes, yes, and check under your door. There's a lot more Selleck where that came from.

Perhaps more than anything, though, you just want to know what to do next. Well, let these two words guide you: *be bold!* You have a human imagination, a gift that no other animal has, and which most breeds of housecat openly covet. The question is whether you have the courage to fantasize *big*.

Think of a beach crowded with thousands and thousands of walruses. All these hulking creatures know of sex is a seasonal blubbery fuckfest—and that works fine for them. But we humans are nourished by variety and starved by stagnation. We die when we commit to any one act or person. If we don't keep moving . . . emotions can . . . it's just very . . . there are times when we tell someone that we love them and they promise to love us in return and we believe it because we *want* to believe it more than *anything*, knowing deep, deep down that she'll never take us with her to Siberia to open a lubricant boutique in a renovated gulag barracks and live happily ever after. We at the Association for the Betterment of Sex thought we were old enough to know better.

Perhaps if there's one thing you should take away from this book, it's this: Dr. Allison Silverman has no intention of marrying you, and waiting for her isn't going to change anything. The human imagination might be great. But damn this human heart!

Also, we didn't devote too much time to anal sex. Some people like it, some don't. Give it a shot.

SELECT BIBLIOGRAPHY

Over the course of the two weeks it took to write this sex manual, ABS consulted the following books, dissertations, and free pamphlets available in urban bus depots. If a source is out of print, find a quiet place to sit and imagine its contents. In no particular order:

PRIMARY SOURCES

Pump and Dump: The Romantic's Guide to Sex

Who Moved My Bowels?

He's Just Not That into You: He's into Your Hotter, Less Whiny Friend

I Love You, You're Perfect, Now Get Off My Face

Bill O'Reilly: Who's Lookin' Out for Your Loofah Zone?

Really, Must You? Sex After 70

Breaking the Yeast Curse with Deepak Chopra

Marriage Counseling the Pol Pot Way

"Monkeys Confused by Jell-O" (YouTube video)

Don't Sweat the Small Stuff (and It's All Small Stuff): Unless You're Reading This in a Burn Unit

Flavor Flav's Illustrated Kama Sutra

The Smell of Garbage, Armpits, and Sadness: Poems

450 Middle-Aged Women Share Anecdotes About Menopause for Some Reason

Serving 25 to Lust: A Guide to Sex Behind Bars, by Ted Travelstead

The Buttafuoco Touch

Drink Yourself Married

Coping with Your Hideous Vagina

Chicken Soup for the Impotent

Mommy and Daddy Are Breaking the Family into Pieces and Ruining Your Life Because They Love You More than Anything: Explaining Divorce to Your Children

Who Moved My Cheese? Seriously? Which One of You Prison Assholes Moved It?

C'mon, Guys, This Isn't Funny Anymore. Anyone Seen My Cheese?

I'm Just Going to Sit Here and Wait Until Someone Returns My Cheese!!!

Piscopo's Guide to Keepin' It Real with da Kidz (ghostwritten)

Aw, Screw It. Anyone Seen My Crackers?

101 Things to Accomplish if You Could Travel Back in Time to the Moment You Began Reading This Book Title

A Friendly Guide to Peeping

"I Am a Highly Successful Internet Entrepreneur with Many Wonderful Friends," and 300 Other Ironclad Pick-Up Techniques for Your 20-Year High-School Reunion

Your Dream Come True! Selling Hand-Crafted Artisan Cock Rings at a Mall Kiosk

Seducing Women with Only Your Guile, Your Positive Attitude, Your Huge Schlong, and $1,000,000 in Cash

Half on the Fridge, Half on the Countertop: And 364 Other Meth-Fueled Sex Positions

What the Bible Says About Pubic Hair

Fundamentals of Grammar and Style (Lifestyle-Slave Edition)

To Even Look upon These Masturbation Techniques Is to Go Mad: Collected Short Stories, by H. P. Lovecraft

Cookin' with Piss, by Emeril Lagasse

Seducing the Blacksmith of Your Dreams

The Pansexual's Guide to the Magic Kingdom

You Just Stiffed Me—Now It's Time for Me to Stiff You: 50 Guaranteed Pickup Lines to Use on Your Waitress

Giving Yourself an Enema the Ancient Native American Way

SECONDARY SOURCES

Would You Like Some Heroin in Exchange for Sex?: The Delicate Art of Seducing Junkies

One Birth Under a Groove: An Extraordinary Guide to Natural Childbirth at Jam-Band Festivals

Everything You Always Wanted to Know About the Opposite Sex but Were Tasered for Asking Previously

Loving What the Hell's Her Name: A Guide for the Parent of the Unexceptional Child

I'm Glad That's Over Already: Overcoming Magnificent Sexual Stamina

The South Coney Island Beach Diet

"I'll Give You Something to Cry About": Dating Insights and Inspiration from America's Leading Alcoholic Dads

Life Sucks: Committing to Cynicism for the Long Haul

Rubble-Dum-Terrys: Sex Games for the Mentally Challenged, by Richard Bannister, M.D.

So You Don't Like Butts, by William Tracy, R.N.

The Great Imam Fatima Hamid, Praise Be His Name, He of the Islamic Republic of Iran, His Honorable Guide to Lovemaking

Dig Ol' Bicks and Pight Tussies: A Dictionary of Sexy Spoonerisms

The Rod Stewart Stomach-Pump Incident: An Oral History

The Good Lord Say "Tap That!": Rationalizing Your Randiness Through Scripture by Creflo A. Dollar

Cockslinger of Congress (The Sexual Years of Lyndon Johnson, Vol. 5), by Robert Caro

Bowel Detoxification the Danny Bonaduce Way

How to Talk to the Opposite Sex Without Brandishing a Weapon

Rum-Tum-Tugging It!: A Photo-Illustrated Guide to Masturbation Techniques, by the Original Broadway Cast of Cats! (Kindle version only)

The Extraordinary Life of Lucky Pierre, by Jean-Michel Guillemin

In Through the Out Door: 101 Classic Rock Albums That Also Sound Like Gay Stuff, by Laura Griffin

Who's Spanking Whom: The Pitfalls of Child Discipline for the Sexually Submissive Parent, by Justice Antonin Scalia

The Pop-Up Book of Genital Warts and Lesions, by Dr. Sadeep Jeevanandam, with "Peanut"

Vasectomies for Dummies

Paul Reiser: The Bootleg Fuck Tape

The History of Erotic Tickling, by Dr. Gavin Newcombe, D.D.S.

How to Work Your Adult Diaper into Casual Conversation

I Think My Pimp Has an Anger Problem

Masturbate Your Way to Success

A Spiritual Solution to That Nasty Rash on Your Inner Thigh

Sorry, Only Happy People Can Get Pregnant

The 4-Minute Workweek: Sell Your Semen and Join the New Rich

SOURCES JUST GLANCED AT FOR A SECOND OR TWO

So, You're Attracted to Grandma

Why Is My Vagina So Hateful?

Prance Away the Gay

Kama Sutra for Impotent Sad Sacks

Killing Mr. Goldfinger: How to Stop Smelling Your Privates in Public

Son, Keep Your Hands Where I Can See 'Em: The Original Screenplay

The Silent Treatment: How to Find Romance by Pretending You're Mute

Discovering the Feminist You, by Dr. Maxxx Poonhound

Now What, Asshole?

ACKNOWLEDGMENTS

SCOTT JACOBSON

Thanks to the Jacobson family, Manoj Viswanathan, Robin Kohli, Jason Reich, and my seventh-grade sex-ed instructor, Mr. Hogan.

TODD LEVIN

Thank you to my family (who I know will be excited to purchase this book, but pray will never read it); my wife, Lisa Whiteman; Bob Powers; Albert Ocampo; and Linda Freeman.

JASON ROEDER

I'd like to thank my family and friends for their steady supply of encouragement. I hope they now understand why I hesitated to talk about this book in great detail.

MIKE SACKS

Thanks and love: Kate and Little D.

TED TRAVELSTEAD

Many thanks and much love to my wife, Julie Wright; my dog, Olive; my incredibly supportive family; Chris Scott; Larry Henry; and all of my fantastic friends.

CREDITS

Robert Sikoryak: viii-ix, xvii-xx (author illustrations throughout), 3, 5, 8, 12, 17, 18, 19, 21, 30, 48, 60, 65, 77, 83, 89, 109, 114-15, 132, 135, 143, 161, 162, 167, 174, 190, 192, 193, 195, 204

Nick Gallo and Michael Faisca: 4, 6, 10, 14, 16, 20, 34, 36, 37, 39, 52, 57, 61, 64, 104, 127, 130, 138, 147, 148, 168, 175, 186, 196, 197 (Machomax supplement), 205–11, 218, 225

David M. Smith, King Power Cinema: 22

Creative Commons: 45

www.b-havior.com: 39

Mr. Kiji: 58–59, 214–16

Juang Jiahui, www.flickr.com/photos/huangjiahui: 62 (Rubik's Cube photo)

Tetra Images: 81

Courtesy of the Library of Congress, LC-B2-2634-1: 98

John Florea/Time&Life Pictures/Getty Images: 131

Emilio Labrador: 159